Contents

Tour de France

Race Facts:

Stage Race

UCI WorldTour

3600km

www.letour.fr

Opposite:
Thousands of fans crowd the course as Lance Armstrong of the USA climbs Alpe d'Huez during the 2004 Tour de France

Like so many great cycle races the grandest of them all, the Tour de France, can trace its routes back to the need to sell newspapers. The Paris – Rouen, established in 1869, had been the work of Richard Lesclide and the Vélocipède Illustrated. In 1891 the Bordeaux – Paris had been sponsored by Véloce Sport under the guidance of Maurice Martin and the great Paris – Brest – Paris had been the creation of Pierre Giffard and his publication Le Petit Journal.

In 1892, Giffard's love of the bicycle resulted in the creation of a new daily sporting journal, Le Vélo. Printed on green paper, the newspaper was an instant success with the sport-mad French public and circulation soared. Then, in 1894, came scandal that would divide a nation.

Alfred Dreyfus, an army officer from the Alsace region of France, was falsely accused of spying for the Germans. His internment on Devils Island lasted until his exoneration in September 1899 but during this time the affair divided a nation. Giffard, a progressive, championed Dreyfus in the pages of Le Vélo, heavily criticising those who considered him a traitor. Unwittingly Giffard found himself censuring those to whom the survival of Le Vélo depended - industrialists such as Michelin, Clément and De Dion whose copious advertising budgets were a great source of income.

Angry with what they saw as a personal attack of the deepest nature De Dion and his colleagues made the decision to establish a journal of their own. L'Auto-Vélo, to be published on yellow paper, was born. Direction of L'Auto-Vélo was placed in the hands of Henri Desgrange, a Parisian journalist and cycling fan who had once been holder of the Hour Record.

However, progressive as it was L'Auto-Vélo suffered from poor circulation – a situation not assisted by an identity crisis following a court order instigated by Giffard instructing that the word Vélo should be removed from the title of the magazine. Something had to be done to increase sales and it had to be done quickly. The idea was to come from one of Desgrange's young journalists, the 23 year old Géo Lefèvre.

And so, on 19 January 1903, L'Auto announced "Le Tour de France, the greatest cycle race in the world".

As the 60 riders lined up at the start of the inaugural Tour on 1 July 1903, none could have imagined the significance of the race on which they were about to embark. Two pre-race favourites had emerged – Maurice Garin and Hippolyte Aucouturier – both of whom had twice won the Queen of Classics, Paris Roubaix. The colossal 467 kilometre first stage from Paris to Lyon was won by Garin in 17 hours 45 minutes. Aucouturier replied by winning the next two stages to take the green armband that indicated the leader of the Tour but his triumph was short lived as he was forced to abandon due to stomach cramps.

first stage. However, chaos reigned as the race progressed through the town of Saint-Etiene where the leading group were held hostage by fans of home-town favourite Antoine Faure until their hero had made good his escape. Only the intervention of a pistol waving Desgrage secured their release. When the race finished in Paris it seemed once more that Garin was triumphant but, on the instructions of the Union Vélocipédique, in investigation into riding irregularities was ordered resulting in the first four competitors being disqualified with 20 year old Henri Cornet being named victor.

It was not until the seventh edition of the tour, held in 1909, that a non-French rider would take victory. Luxembourgian François Faber took five straight stage wins, a record unbroken to this day, wearing the leader's armband from the end of the second stage to the race finish 3818 kilometres later.

Garin retained the lead to take the next two stages and overall victory at the Parc de Princes. Only 24 riders finished the inaugural Tour, the last finishing with a deficit of 2 days, 16 hours, 47 minutes and 22 seconds.

Favourite to win the tour in its second outing, Garin lived up to expectations by once again winning the

In 1910 the tour strayed into the mountains for the first time, despite protestations from some of the riders who were convinced they would wither be eaten by bears or die trying to reach the summits. The riders took on some of the toughest climbs of the Pyrenees

Above: *Portrait of Italian cyclist Ottavio Bottecchia winner of the Tour de France in 1924 and 1925*

Christophe. Riding the sixth stage from Bayonne to Luchon, the young Frenchman had lead the field over the climb of the Col d'Aubisque and ascended the Tourmalet in style. Disaster struck descending on the poorly constructed mountain roads and without warning the fork on his cycle broke. As was the custom with cycle racing at this time, the rules prevented any external intervention or support – it would be many years before riders enjoyed the comfort of a mechanic following in a team car. Determined to continue, Christophe walked 14 kilometres to the village of Sainte-Marie-de-Campan where, on being directed to the local blacksmiths forge, he proceeded to braze and repair his own machine under the watchful gaze of Tour officials before rejoining the race several hours in arrears. For his trouble, Christophe was handed an additional time penalty for allowing a young boy to pump the bellows of the forge whilst he worked.

Interrupted by the horrors of the First World War, the Tour de France returned to the racing calendar in the summer of 1919 with a new innovation that would become the race's greatest icon, the maillot jaune. Coloured yellow

and the Tourmalet, Aspin, Peyresourde and Aubisque were introduced to Tour folklore.

Further folklore was created at the 1913 Tour by 28 year old Eugene

in recognition of the pages of L'Auto its first recipient was none other that Eugene Christophe. Having led the race from stage four, Christophe looked almost certain to win but on the penultimate stage from Metz to Dunkerque history repeated itself and his forks broke allowing Belgian Firmin Lambot to take the lead and the overall victory.

Belgian Philippe Thys set a record in 1920 by becoming the first rider to win three Tours de France, a record that would not be equalled for another thirty years.

The 1924 Tour was won in the greatest style by Italian climber Ottavio Bottecchia. Donning the yellow jersey after winning the first 381 kilometre stage from Paris to Le Havre he continued to wear it, singing as he pedalled, for the remaining 5,044 kilometres back to Paris twenty-seven days later.

Henri Desgrange was always looking for new ways to challenge the mettle of the competitors. It seemed that no obstacle would be considered too tough to endure and so, in 1927, a new format was introduced. Riders continued to contest mountain stages in company but were forced to ride flat stages individually or in the company of their own team. All of a sudden the nature of the race had changed and the long stages no longer offered any respite or rest instead becoming 200 kilometre team time trials.

The revised format was a disaster and by the time the race returned to Paris, 103 of the 142 starter had abandoned. In an admission of error, the Tour was returned to its traditional format just two years later in 1929. However, this would

Below: *Eugene Christophe one of France's greatest racing cyclists*

that time bonuses of four, three and two minutes would be awarded for first, second and third places on each stage. Furthermore if a rider should finish more than three minutes clear he would gain an additional three minutes. Not surprisingly it was found that this system favoured the sprinters of the peleton so to create a balance Desgrange introduced a new competition, the King of the Mountains, in 1933 with points being awarded to the first riders to crest the summits of the greatest climbs.

A new invention was used in 1937 that would transform the race for ever. The introduction of the derailleur gear all but won the Tour for French hero Roger Lapébie allowing him to turn an enormous gear on the fast flat road but still have a smaller climbing gear in reserve for the hills.

A new star had come to light in the 1937 tour in the form of reigning Giro d'Italia champion Gino Bartali. Sailing over the hallowed Col du Galibier he had won the stage from Aix-les-Bains to Grenoble and in doing so taken the yellow jersey although an early retirement due to fever prevented him from taking overall victory. However, Bartali reversed his misfortune the

not prevent Desgrange from continuing to tamper with the structure of the race and in 1930 a new idea was introduced that would stay in place until 1968, with the race being contested by national teams.

Having abolished the participation of commercially sponsored teams the organisers of the tour were required to look for new sources of revenue. A scheme was devised whereby businesses could finance a part of the Tour in return for having their goods promoted along the route and so the Caravane publicitaire was born.

Yet another amendment to the rules was made in 1932. In an attempt to increase combativity it was announced

following year when he took victory by over 18 minutes from Belgian Félicien Vervaecke following a defining Alpine ride from Digne to Briançon.

During the Second World War the German occupying forces had wanted the Tour to continue without interruption but their request was refused by Jacques Goddet who had taken over as editor of L'Auto and organiser of the Tour following the death of Henri Desgrange in 1940. However, as the nation emerged from conflict it became obvious that the return of Tour de France was not just desired but needed by a French public desperate for a distraction from the years of Nazi rule. France got its Tour and with it a French victor in the form of the diminutive Jean Robic competing in his first ever Tour de France for the West France regional team.

Gino Bartali returned to the Tour in 1938, ten years after his first victory. Although much lauded, at 34 years old few considered him a serious contender for overall honours. Opinions were changed on the first stage when the Italian took victory and the yellow jersey but the early lead was soon lost following a crash the next day. Despite winning two stages in the Pyrenees, for many it looked as if Bartali's chances were reduced to zero. However, Bartali had other ideas and three back to back stage wins in the Alps catapulted him back into a yellow jersey that he would wear all the way to Paris.

Having twice won the Giro d'Italia, Fausto Coppi's arrival at the 1949 Tour de France was greeted with eager anticipation with the Italian nation was clearly split in its loyalties – the devoutly religious Bartali appealed to the traditional agricultural south whilst the young secular Coppi was the darling of the modern industrial north. Italian directeur sportif Alfredo Binda had worked wonders in securing the services of both riders and, with a pact agreed, they promised to set aside their rivalries.

Coppi started the race in a disastrous fashion, crashing and destroying his bike on the fifth stage and only the intervention of Binda prevented him from packing up and returning home

early. Fortunes began to change when he won the 92 kilometre time trial to La Rochelle at the beginning of the second week and further gains were made as the race progressed through the Pyrenees. Then, on entering the Alps, Bartali and Coppi launched a successful attack on the slopes of the Col d'Izoard – Bartali was once again in the familiar yellow jersey. The pair attacked again the following day but Bartali punctured on the fast descent from the Petit Saint-Bernard pass. Encouraged by Binda, Coppi pressed on alone to take the stage and control of the race – a position he consolidated three days later by winning the 137 kilometre time-trial to Nancy. On reaching Paris, Coppi had become the first person to win both the Giro and the Tour in the same year.

Coppi returned to Tour de France glory in 1952 following intervening wins for Swiss stars Ferdi Kübler and Hugo Koblet. In the first year that the race enjoyed television coverage Coppi reigned supreme, taking charge on the tenth stage as it wound its way to the ski station at L'Alpe d'Huez. The following day Coppi broke clear again. Riding solo on the final climb to Sestrières alone he had increased his general classification

Above: *Jacques Anquetil (right) who won the 1964 Tour de France for the fifth time is congratulated by second place winner Raymond Poulidor July 1964*

Bobet was neither a natural climber nor sprinter but through sheer determination he taught himself to do both with the best. Between 1953 and 1955 the entire French nation was set alight by the Tour de France exploits of the Breton who became the first rider to win the race in three consecutive years.

Bobet announced whilst riding the 1957 Giro d'Italia that he would not contest that year's Tour de France. Replacements were hurriedly found in the form of André Darrigarde and a 23 year old professional called Jacques Anquetil. Winning the fourth stage as the Tour rolled into his home town of Rouen, Anquetil was suddenly thrown into the limelight and the yellow jersey. He lost control two days later but proved his worth as the race entered the Alps, climbing like no other to regain the maillot jaune. A dominating performance in the final time trial from Bordeaux to Libourne sealed a notable victory for the young star but his true greatness was to come four years later.

Following victories by Luxembourgian Charly Gaul and the Eagle of Toledo, Federico Bahamontes - gifted by the in-squabbling of the French team - Anquetil returned to Tour greatness in

lead to almost 20 minutes and secured his second tour victory.

Having held the maillot jaune for eight days in the 1948 Tour only to be robbed by Gino Bartali as the race headed to Aix-les-Bains, Louison Bobet had gone on to take victory in Paris – Nice, Milan Sanremo and Giro di Lombardia.

1961. Derrigade won the opening road stage but, with an individual time trial contested on the same day, his spell in the yellow jersey was limited to just a few hours before Anquetil took over as race leader. Untouchable for the entire race, his lead was never challenged and twenty days later as the peleton entered Paris Anquetil had secured his second Tour victory.

Anquetil added to his 1957 and 1961 victories with three further triumphs in 1962 and 1963 to become the first rider to win the Tour on four occasions and then again in 1964 to make take his tally to five. This final victory was in many respects his greatest as he battled tooth and nail with his greatest rival Raymond Poulidor. Having just secured his second Giro d'Italia, Anquetil remained unseen for the first week as his German Saint-Raphaël team mate first took the green points jersey and then the maillot jaune on the fifth stage into Fribourg-en-Brisgau. It was only when the race arrived at the Alps that it became apparent how much Anquetil was suffering. As the attacks came he could do nothing to respond, finding it difficult even to keep down the iced water handed to him by his directeur sportif. The following day

provided some kind of respite as a weary peleton headed for Monaco. Anquetil, known for his powers of recovery, seized his chance as the riders approached the cinder track finish out-sprinting Briton Tom Simpson to win the stage.

A second stage win was forthcoming in the time trial the following day and suddenly Anquetil, who had considered abandoning just two days before, was sitting in second place behind compatriot

Below: *British roadracing cyclist and first British world professional cycling champion Tommy Simpson*

Above: *Yellow jersey leader Eddy Merckx (left) rides uphill with Frenchman Raymond Poulidor during the 10th stage of the Tour de France, July 1974*

Georges Groussard with Poulidor a further 30 seconds in arrears. Anquetil finally asserted his control on the stage 17 time-trial to Bayonne by winning the stage and taking the leaders jersey. When the race reached the Puy de Dôme Anquetil's lead over Poulidor was a slim 56 seconds. The two climbed side by side until Anquetil cracked allowing Poulidor to ride away. The Champion pressed on and, despite loosing 42 seconds in the final 600 metres, nothing could be done to unseat Anquetil from a fifth Tour victory.

16   LITTLE BOOK OF **CYCLE RACING**

For Frenchman Roger Pingeon, completing the 1967 Tour should have been a joyous moment. He had taken the maillot jaune after winning the fifth stage from Amiens to Roubaix and for all but one day had ridden resplendent in its colour. But the tour arrived in mourning having lost one of its own on the slopes of Mont Ventoux. British rider Tom Simpson was one of the most popular riders in the peleton with a palmares that included the World Championship, Tour of Flanders and Milan Sanremo. Simpson, Poulidor and eventual stage winner Julio Jiménez were amongst the first to attack as the riders approached the final climb. At first his effort was strong and purposeful but as he progressed his riding became slow and weary. He started weaving from side to side and then, without warning he collapsed by the side of the road. Spectators helped him remount and he pressed on but he collapsed again. His autopsy showed he had enormous amounts of amphetamine in his body. At last the issues of doping in professional cycle racing were out in the open.

Eddy Merckx made no secret of the fact he intended to win the Tour at his first attempt in 1969 and who would dare argue with him? At 24 years old his palmares already included the World Championship, Giro d'Italia, Paris-Nice, Paris-Roubaix, Liége-Bastogne-Liége and two wins of Milan-Sanremo. However, Merckx's preparation had been flawed. Competing in the Giro he had tested positive for amphetamines and been expelled. Although his name was subsequently cleared he had lost 18 days of racing.

Before the race was a week old Merckx had already won two stages and was wearing the yellow jersey. He continued to stamp his authority by humiliating his two strongest challengers, Italian Felice Gimondi and one-time Anquetil sparring partner Raymond Poulidor, by comprehensively dropping them on the slopes of the Ballon d'Alsace. In a class of his own, Merckx was never once troubled on the way to his first Tour de France.

Having watched Merckx win the 1970 Giro d'Italia the peleton returned to Tour resigned that they were competing for second place. The Belgian immediately opened his account by winning the prologue time trial but remained unconcerned when two days later Italo Zilioli moved into yellow.

Moving back into control on stage six, his mortality was only challenged on the lunar landscape of the Ventoux where he won the stage but collapsed afterward whist conducting a press conference.

In 1971 Merckx found himself challenged for the first time. The Tour opened in predictable fashion with Merckx winning the prologue and taking the yellow jersey but constant attacks from climbers Bernard Thévenet of France and Spaniard Luis Ocaña increased the pressure until, on the Puy de Dôme, he cracked. Ocaña attacked again on the Alpine stage from Orcières to Merlette gaining nine minutes to take the maillot jaune as the Belgian struggled below. Merckx new he had to act and at the next day he attacked from the start. A precious two minutes were recouped but there was still everything to play for. As the race moved into the Pyrenees the weather took a turn for the worse and the peleton was hit by heavy rain and storm. Merckx attacked again and again but Ocaña bravely hung on to his lead. Then disaster struck the young Spaniard. Unable to make a hairpin turn whilst descending the Col de Mente, he overshot and plunged into a ravine. In excruciating pain and unable to continue

Ocaña was airlifted from the mountain. Merckx was back in yellow but as a mark of respect for his adversary he refused to wear the maillot jaune the next day. His only opponent removed from the frame, Merckx continued the race untroubled to take his third consecutive victory.

A great deal of anticipation greeted the start of the 1972 Tour. Merckx and Ocaña were expecting a battle royal but, after the Belgian won the prologue, their collective thunder was stolen by Frenchman Cyril Guimard of the Gan team who took the sprint on the first stage and with it the yellow jersey. Although still leading at the end of the first week Guimard started to suffer with knee pains that got progressively worse. With doctors diagnosing water on the knee the brave Frenchman could only continue with the aid of daily injections of Novocaine. After battling bravely across the Pyrenees, Guimard made it to the Alps before abandoning in tears. By this point the Merckx – Ocaña battle was already over, the Spaniard having crashed once again on a Pyrenean descent. From taking the yellow jersey on the eighth stage to Luchon, Merckx remained untroubled in his quest for a fourth. Standing on the podium in Paris,

Merckx made a sporting gesture to an emotional Guimard by presenting him with his green jersey.

Deciding not to contest the 1973 Tour, Merckx instead concentrated on the Giro and Vuelta but for Ocaña it was the opportunity he had been waiting for. This year he avoided careless accidents on the way to taking his first Tour victory

Above: *Bernard Hinault of France in action*

but 37 year old Raymond Poulidor was not so fortunate. Whilst descending the Portet d'Aspet the Frenchman lost control plunging headfirst into a ravine.

Merckx returned for his fifth Tour de France in 1974 recovering from an operation. Many thought his performance would be affected but the Cannibal had other ideas as he proceeded to collect as many points as he could in

LITTLE BOOK OF **CYCLE RACING**

the first week before taking the first two consecutive Alpine stages. Once again he was unstoppable and after nineteen days in yellow he triumphantly sprinted to his thirty-second stage win and fifth Tour de France victory in Paris.

The route of the 1977 Tour employed shock tactics by sending the peleton into the Pyrenees on just the second day. Bernard Thévenet took the victory after taking control after the 14 kilometre mountain time-trial from Morzine to Avoriaz from German Dietrich Thurau who had worn yellow since the prologue in Fleurance eighteen days earlier. Thévenet's win was, however, tainted with allegations of drug taking which he later admitted.

Bernard Hinault's victory in 1978 would be the first of many. The reign of Eddy Merckx was at an end after he had finished sixth the previous year and it was a time for young blood to come to the fore. Hinault, known to many as The Badger, had already shown his worth in the Spring Classics and was regarded as a fine rider against the watch. His credentials as a Tour contender were confirmed when won the mountainous Dauphiné Libéré. Always in touch with the action the young Frenchman excelled

in the mountains but it was not until the final time-trial from Metz to Nancy that he took the yellow jersey from Dutch race leader Joop Zoetemelk, beating him by over four minutes over 72 kilometres.

The Zoetemelk – Hinault battle returned the following year and once again victory would fall to the Frenchman after a dominating display in the 54 kilometre stage 15 mountain time-trial from Évian to the ski station at Avoriaz. On the final day, as the peleton swept along the cobbles of the Champs-Élysées, Zoetemelk launched a final attack but Hinault responded and the two riders sprinted for the stage win with Hinault taking glory.

Zootemelk, riding for Ti-Raleigh, finally got his Tour de France victory in 1979. In a race battered by appalling weather conditions Hinault abandoned on the thirteenth stage suffering with tendonitis. Zootemelk, poised in second place, inherited the jersey and stamped his authority on the race by winning the final Saint Etienne time trial.

Hinault returned to take consecutive victories in 1981 and a 1982 Tour interrupted by demonstrations by protesting French farmers. Using his superlative ability against the clock

Above: *Marco Pantani on the podium of the 20th stage of the Tour de France in Le Creusot, 1998*

riding for the same Renault team. Like Hinault, Fignon was a brilliant climber and a stylish time-trialist – attributes that were fast becoming essential for any serious hope of tour success. Consistent riding from the first stage kept Fignon in contention, something he capitalised on as the race headed to the dizzy heights of L'Alpe d'Huez. Escaping with a select group including Lucien Van Impe and Spaniard Pedro Delgado, he finished in the second group but climbed into yellow. To confirm his status as a worthy champion Fignon completed his tour with an elegant time-trial victory on the roads of Dijon.

Hinault returned to the Tour in 1984 having joined the new La Vie Claire squad. Fignon arrived as French National Champion fresh from the Giro d'Italia having only lost the lead to Francesco Moser on the final stage. For a moment it looked like business as usual as The Badger took victory in the prologue time-trial, three seconds ahead of Fignon. But Fignon fought back, first in the team time-trial as part of the winning Renault –Elf team and then in all three individual time-trials. However, it was once again on the slopes of L'Alpe d'Huez that Fignon would take control

Hinault was again unstoppable, gaining the maillot jaune on the stage to Pau in 1981 and on at Valence d'Agen in 1982, both mountain time-trials.

With Hinault sidelined through injury the 1983 Tours was won by a young Frenchman, Laurent Fignon, of the yellow jersey on a stage won by Columbian national team rider Lucho Herrera, the only amateur ever to win a stage of the Tour de France. Fignon maintained his lead to Paris to take his second tour victory in front of an ecstatic and partisan French crowd.

The next year it was Fignon who was sidelined as he recovered from an Achilles tendon operation. It was once again Hinault's turn to shine. Briefly wearing yellow after winning the prologue, Hinault finally took control of the lead on the eighth stage time-trial to Strasbourg and stayed in the maillot jaune all the way to Paris to become the third rider to win the Tour of five occasions.

Many expected Hinault to take a sixth tour in 1986 and as he collected the yellow jersey at the end of the twelfth stage from Bayonne to Pau it seemed a likely outcome but they had not counted on the actions of his young lieutenant, the American Greg Lemond. Lemond took the maillot jaune from his captain on the stage seventeen climb of the Col du Granon. However, Lemond was more than aware of his leader's ambitions and his concerns were proved founded when the next day, on the descent off

the Col du Galibier, Hinault escaped in a last ditch attempt for glory. Lemond responded and, assisted by Canadian Stever Bauer bridged the gap. An exhausted Bauer was soon dropped and leaving the two La Vie Claire riders to

Below: *Dutch cyclist Joop Zoetemelk with the trophy for winning the Tour de France presented by Jacques Chirac, July 1980*

of opportunity. Hinault had retired and Lemond was absent having been involved in a hunting accident. Even Laurent Fignon was not considered a threat having displayed poor form throughout the year. That year victory fell to 27 year old Irishman Stephen Roche who first took the yellow jersey on the road to Villard-de-Lans before losing it the next day to Pedro Delgado by just 21 seconds. Unable to break clear from the Spaniard through the Alps, Roche new his only chance was the final 38 kilometre individual time-trial at Dijon on the penultimate day of the Tour. Jean-Françoise Bernard won the stage but Roche had done enough to take the maillot jaune by 40 seconds.

Pedro Delgado took victory the following year with a victory tainted by accusations of drug taking. On ten occasions he tested positive for probenicid a drug which in itself had no performance enhancing properties but was used as a masking agent for anabolic steroids. Whilst the substance appeared in the International Olympic Committee's banned list the UCI had failed to update their records and as such Delgado had committed no offence.

Delgado's attempt at a second Tour

crest the Croix-de-Fer alone. There then followed an extraordinary display as the old hand paced the young pretender up the final ascent of L'Alpe d'Huez. Hinault eased to cross the line level with Lemond but the American pushed him forward to take the stage in the knowledge that he had already won the Tour.

The 1987 Tour was seen as a tour

victory went wrong before the race had even started when he missed his allotted prologue start time whilst signing autographs. French hopes were pinned on Fignon whose return to form was welcomed by a nation. Nobody really expected that Lemond, back in action having recovered from his gunshot wounds, could take a second Tour, however, a victory in the stage five time trial found him unexpectedly back in yellow. Fignon responded on the tenth stage climb of Superbagnères and, to many, it looked as if the Frenchman would take the Tour. Unbeaten, Lemond regained the lead in the mountain time-trial to Orcières Merlette, increasing his advantage further the next day as the race swept across the Alps to Briançon. Finally, on the seventeenth stage, Fignon successfully attacked on the road to L'Alpe d'Huez and by the time the Tour arrived at Versailles four days later for the start of the final time-trial to Paris the Frenchman had an advantage of 50 seconds over Lemond.

Lemond took to the star on a low-profile cycle equipped with a disc wheel, aerodynamic helmet and a new innovation, the triathlon handlebar. Fignon had the specialist bike but no

aerodynamic aids. Pedalling smoothly, Lemond made swift progress on the 24.5 kilometres to Paris. Arriving first at the finish all he could do was wait for his adversary to appear. As the time checks came in it was obvious that Lemond was faster but was he fast enough? As Fignon crossed the finish line the result was confirmed. Lemond had won his second tour by just eight seconds.

The following year Lemond made it three. Having tracked the main protagonists for the course of the race the American moved into contention as the race climbed to the summit at Luz Ardiden on a stage won by a young domestique called Miguel Induráin. Lemond had slipped into second place, just five seconds behind Italian race leader Claudio Chiappucci. Four days later, in the final time-trial, the trap was sprung and, by taking second place, Lemond was once again wearer of the maillot jaune and winner of the Tour de France.

The 1991 Tour signalled the start of a new reign, that of Miguel Induráin. Induráin an athlete of phenomenal physical attributes, in the world of Lance Armstrong "a freak of nature". His resting pulse rate was 29 beats per minute and his lung capacity eight litres compare to an average fit human at 50 to 60 beats per minute and a mere five litre capacity. Tall an immensely powerful he was considered the ultimate Tour-winning machine.

Induráin took his inaugural yellow jersey in the company of Claudio Chiappucci on the stage to Val Louron having dropped Greg Lemond and race leader Luc Leblanc on the climb of the Tourmalet. With no intention of relinquishing his lead Indurain defended the maillot jaune like a seasoned Tour winner all the way to Paris. In the final sprint on the Champs Élysées, Djamolidine Abdoujaparov, an Uzbek sprinter known as the Tashkent Terror, crashed after hitting a metal barrier. By crossing the finish line on foot fifteen minutes after the peleton and aided by a doctor he secured his title as winner of the Green Jersey point competition.

For the next four years the focus of the Tour was not so much who would win but when would Indurain take control. Almost unbeatable against the watch and capable of climbing with the best his metronomic style and emotionless expression were like a hallmark to the Tour.

In 1992 Induráin's only serious adversary was his climbing partner from the previous year, Claudio Chiappucci. In a brave, perhaps foolhardy, attack the diminutive Italian slipped free of the peleton after crossing the Mont Cenis pass on the road to the classic stage finish at Sestrières. Although a solo break of 200 kilometres won Chiappucci the stage, Indurain crossed the line just 1'45" behind to take the yellow jersey en route to a second Tour victory.

Induráin's domination of the 1993 tour was almost complete. Taking

Above: *Miguel Induráin and the rest of the peloton pass in front of the Champs Elysees during the 20th and last stage of the Tour de France. Induráin won the event for the third straight time*

Opposite: *Miguel Induráin of Spain on his way to victory in stage 19 around lake de Vassiviere in Auphelle, France*

Above: *Chris Boardman in action in the first time trial stage of the 1994 Tour de France. Boardman finished in first place to become the first Briton to take the yellow jersey since Tommy Simpson in 1962*

challenge to Induráin's dominance – Tony Rominger of Switzerland – who achieved consecutive stage wins as the race swept across the Alps and victory in the final time-trial to finish second on the podium in Paris.

Riding in his first Tour de France, British Olympic star Chris Boardman took victory in the 1994 prologue time trial distancing Induráin by 7 seconds, a huge margin over a 7.2 kilometre course. The next day, as the race speed through the street of Armentières, an horrific crash caused by a photo-taking Gendarme caused the early retirement of Belgian sprinter Wilfred Neilssen and French hope Laurent Jalabert. In an exciting excursion from mainland Europe the Tour crossed the English Channel for two stages in the United Kingdom – the first from Dover to Brighton followed by a circuit from Portsmouth taking in the Hampshire countryside. For Induráin it was business as usual at the stage nine time-trial. Finishing with a two minute advantage over second placed Rominger he was back in yellow once again and a fourth victory was a mere formality.

1995 will be remembered as a dark year for the Tour de France. As the race traversed the Pyrenees on stage fifteen

yellow in the Puy-du-Fou prologue time trial, he relinquished control only for the sprinters to take their glory in the opening week. By the end of the stage nine individual time-trial he was back in yellow but not before a 21 year old Lance Armstrong had become the youngest post-war stage winner by taking victory in Verdun. Just one rider had posed a

Italian Fabio Casartelli, winner of the Olympic Road Race in 1992, lost control and crashed heavily on the descent of the Portet d'Aspet striking his head heavily on a concrete bollard. Tended at the roadside by race doctors, he was immediately airlifted to a local hospital here he arrested and died that afternoon. As a mark of respect the following stage to Pau was ridden in complete silence with Casartelli's Motorola team mates crossing the finish line-abreast. The stage was declared null and void. Two days later, Motorola team leader Lance Armstrong took an emotional stage victory at Limoges pointing to the sky as

a tribute to his fallen colleague.

Indurain took his fifth Tour de France to match the feats of Anquetil, Merckx and Hinault but once again a great reign was about to some to an end.

The seventh stage of the 1996 Tour has gone down as one of the defining moments in Tour history for it was here that the Miguel Indurain phenomenon came to an end. In lashing rain Frenchman Stéphane Heulot had abandoned, Johan Bruyneel had crashed, so had Alex Zülle, twice, and Laurent Jalabert had been dropped as the remains of a depleted and demoralised peleton drifted its way from Chambéry through the Alps to Les

Below: Fans watch as riders climb past the monument honoring Fabio Casartelli, who died during a crash on this route in 1995

Above: *Bjarne Riis of Denmark wins stage nine and takes the yellow jersey during the Tour De France in 1996*

Opposite: *Jan Ullrich of Germany raises his arms while standing on the final podium in Paris*

Riis of the Deutsche Telekom team who took control of the race after winning the 46 kilometre ninth stage that had been shortened due to heavy snowfall on the Col du Galibier. On taking the honours in Paris, only the time-trialing ability of his young German team mate, Jan Ullrich, had looked capable of derailing his plans.

When Jan Ullrich took victory in the 1997 Tour many expected the start of a reign to rival or even surpass Induráin. Boardman once more took victory in the Prologue but the German was in second place, distanced by a mere 2 seconds. Consecutive stage wins by the self proclaimed fastest man on earth, Mario Cipollini, saw the jersey rest on the shoulders of the Italian sprinter for much of the first week only to taken on stage five by Frenchman Cédric Vasseur following a 140 kilometre lone break. Vasseur retained the jersey until, as the race strayed into the Principality of Andorra, Ulrich took command by destroying a fragmented peleton on the climb to Arcalis. Only French climber Richard Virenque could trouble the German as the race headed into the Alps, his team launching constant attacks to wear the race leader down. But Ullrich

Arcs. Then, almost within sight of the stage finish, Indurain cracked for the first time. His once super-cool demeanour now showed an expression of agony as he crawled his way to finish the stage over four minutes down on winner Luc Leblanc. He, and his adversaries, new that this year's Tour would herald a new winner.

That winner was to be Dane Bjarne

could not be fazed and as Tour finished in Paris the first German winner was crowned victorious.

As the prologue of the 1998 tour commenced in Dublin, a Festina soigneur by the name of Willy Voet was held in custody by the French police having been stopped crossing the border from Belgium in a team car stocked full of performance enhancing drugs bound for the Tour. Six days into the tour Richard Virenque and the Festina team, still protesting their innocence, were expelled in disgrace. A tidal wave of protests, suspensions and abandons followed that threatened the very Tour itself as ONCE, Banesto, TVM, Kelme and Vitalicio Seguros withdrew en-masse.

In spite of the difficulties a race developed sparked by Jan Ullrich's victory in the stage seven time-trial. The German's time in yellow was initially short lived as Laurent Desbiens briefly took control but a solid performance on the climb to Luchon returned it to the shoulders of the Telekom star. Although many thought that Ullrich would wear yellow to Paris, it seemed that Italian climber Marco Pantani had different plans. Attacking in devastating fashion

over the Galibier before dropping his opponent on the climb to Les Deux Alpes, the wiry Italian had catapulted himself into a maillot jaune he would continue to wear to the Champs Élysées.

As the new millennium approached, cycle racing, and in particular the Tour de France, needed a saviour. Damaged by the Festina Affair, almost to breaking point, something special was needed to put the sport back on track in the eyes of the riders, the sponsors and the fans. That something was to be Lance Armstrong.

Armstrong's story is familiar to most. The youngest ever winner of the World Road Championship, winner of two Tour de France stages, winner of the San Sebastian Classic and Flèche Wallonne – the future looked promising for this rising Texas star. But then a bombshell hit as Armstrong was diagnosed with testicular cancer with tumours on his lungs and abdomen and lesions on his Briain. His chances of survival were slim, his chances of recovery less. But with typically characteristic determination and resolve, recover he did.

The Texan arrived at the 1998 Tour a very different rider to the one that had ridden in 1995. His physique had changed immeasurably from a stocky 80 kilogram powerhouse to a svelte 72 kilogram tour contender. His riding style had also changed, his pedalling rate increasing from 85 revolutions pre minute to a lightning 105. He immediately made an impact by winning

the prologue time-trial by seven seconds from Alex Zülle.

Attentions briefly turned to the Lion King, Mario Cipollini, who, in a first week packed with sprints, won four consecutive stages, setting a record speed of 50.355 km/h in the 191 kilometre stage to Blois. Armstrong reclaimed the yellow jersey at the first individual time-trial after handing out a 58 second beating to Zülle with third placed Christophe Moreau a further 67 seconds in arrears. As if not satisfied with proving his worth in the time-trials, Armstrong administered a fatal blow to his opponents the very next day by taking a solo victory on the climb to Sestrières to lead the Tour by over six minutes. Armstrong lead was never challenged, his only rival Zülle having lost time in a crash on stage two. With victory further sealed by another model performance in the final time-trial at Futuroscope, Armstrong rode to the finish Champion of the Tour de France.

In a surprise result, the prologue of the millennium Tour was won by Scotland's David Millar competing in his first Tour de France with Armstrong two seconds behind. Millar held the yellow jersey for two more days before first Jalabert and then Alberto Elli took

control. Others may have had designs on a Tour de France victory but it was once again Armstrong who delivered after taking control on the first mountain stage to Hautacam. Spaniard Javier Otxoa was already ahead on a solo

Left: *Italian cyclist Marco Pantani sitting on the road during the Tour de France cyclists' demonstration at the beginning of the 12th stage in Tarascon-sur- Ariege, in a protest against the media's coverage of the race concentrating on doping affairs*

break when Pantani launched his attack. Armstrong's response was crushing as he first chased down Pantani and then, without breaking cadence, rode past him and out of sight to finish second place on the stage, just 42 seconds behind escapee Otxoa, and claim another yellow jersey. Armstrong was attacked again and again as the race progressed through the Alps but although Pantani could offer a worthy fight, the lead was never seriously challenged.

Jan Ullrich's form at the 2001 Tour was as good it ever had been, but it was still not enough to deny Armstrong of a third consecutive victory. Once again, Armstrong took control of the race in the Pyrenees on a stage which crossed the Portet d'Aspet, scene of Fabio Casartelli's tragic 1995 death. Having spent most of the day in a break with rival Jan Ulrich, Armstrong once again attacked on the final climb to take victory as the German looked helplessly on.

With Ulrich sidelined through injury it seemed as if there was nobody capable of contesting Armstrong's superiority at the 2002 Tour. Taking no unnecessary risks, by the time Armstrong left the Alps bound for Paris, a fourth tour was already his.

LITTLE BOOK OF **CYCLE RACING**

Constantly marked and attacked by all the leaders, the Centenary 2003 Tour was the hardest fought for Armstrong. Finishing seventh in the prologue time trial behind, amongst others, Jan Ullrich and CSC rider Tyler Hamilton, he had failed to deal his customary opening psychological blow. However, normality returned to the Armstrong camp as a third place on the climb to L'Alpe d'Huez secured the maillot jaune once more. Armstrong's cool in the face of adversity became apparent the next day when Kazak Alexander Vinokourov escaped the leaders on the descent into Gap. During the ensuing chase, ONCE leader Joseba Beloki crashed just metres in front of the fast moving Armstrong. For all the world it looked as if Armstrong would go down also, but in an amazing display of bike handling he freewheeled off the road and down a hillside to meet his fellow pursuers as they sped past.

Ullrich's performance in the stage twelve time trial put Armstrong under yet more pressure. His 1'34" beating of the American had placed him just 34 second in arrears on general classification with eight stages remaining. The following day the attacks came thick and fast allowing Ulrich to drop Armstrong in the final kilometres of the climb to Plateau de Bonascre. Armstrong responded to limit the damage but Ulrich had clawed himself yet closer as the margin dropped to just 15 seconds. Drama unfolded once more on the climb of the Luz Ardiden as Armstrong was felled having caught his handlebars in a spectator's bag bringing down Iban Mayo in the process. Although it could have won him the Tour de France, Ulrich refused to take advantage, waiting for Armstrong to recover before he again picked up the pace. As the race approached the summit Armstrong attacked again, riding into the mist to secure a stage win and to deny Ulrich a valuable time bonus. Only as he completed the rain-soaked final time trial from Pornic to Nantes did Armstrong know that his fifth Tour victory was secure. He had at last matched the achievements of Anquetil, Merckx, Hinault and Indurain.

A new Tour and a new challenge appeared for Armstrong in 2004 as he ventured into the unknown in an attempt to win his sixth successive Tour de France. The first week of competition brought to the fore an unexpected race leader in French National Champion Thomas Voeckler after a stage five

Opposite: *Alex Zulle in action*

break on the road to Chartres. Voeckler gallantly defended his lead for ten days until Armstrong and Ivan Basso escaped on the stage to Villard de Lans. Armstrong strengthened his lead with two astounding time trial performances both won with margins in excess of one minute. Taking to the podium on the Champs Élysées, Armstrong had gone one better than any other rider in history and taken a sixth Tour. Joining Armstrong on the podium, Frenchman Richard Virenque set a record of his own in taking his seventh victory in the King of the Mountains competition.

Armstrong's seventh and final Tour victory opened with a second place behind new super-fast time-trialist, David Zabriske of the CSC team. However, he only had to wait for the stage four team time-trial from Tours to Blois to don the yellow jersey for the first time as his Discovery Channel Team stormed around the 67.5 kilometre course at an average speed of 57.31 km/h, a record for a Tour de France stage. Undefended by Armstrong, at the end of a tough stage nine from Gérardmer to Mulhouse the leader's jersey had moved to the shoulders of Germany's Jens Voight of CSC but only for a day. Another newcomer to

the Tour, Spaniard Alejandro Valverde of the Illes Balears team set his stall for future Tour de France fame by winning the hallowed stage to Courchavel in the company of Armstrong who, once again, took control of the maillot jaune. Despite his best efforts, second placed Ivan Basso could do nothing to wrestle the yellow jersey from Armstrong's vice like grip. Armstrong had achieved the unthinkable and won an amazing seventh Tour de France.

Little did the cycling world know, that Tour de France history was about to be shattered seven years later. Following his retirement in 2011 – he returned to the race and finished third in the 2009 Tour – Armstrong was facing doping allegations and in June the following year USADA, the US anti-doping agency, duly charged the Texan. That August, he was issued with a lifetime ban, the agency's damning report highlighting that Armstrong was involved in the "the most sophisticated, professionalized and successful doping program that sport has ever seen."

In December 2013, he finally admitted to doping during a television interview conducted by Oprah Winfrey.

You only have to peruse the Tour

record books – there is a blank set of results from 1999-2005 – to understand the humiliation Armstrong poured over the sport in those years. Yet, despite Armstrong being found guilty, the dirty past of the Tour still came back to haunt the 100th edition of the race, when Armstrong told French newspaper Le Monde that he couldn't have won without doping and that he felt he was still the winner of the 1999-2005 races.

Rewind the clock and the winner of the 2006 Tour was hard to decipher, with Armstrong now retired from the saddle. Ironically, considering the damage Armstrong was to do the sport in future years, the race was won by Floyd Landis, while the event was marred by several doping allegations. Ullrich and Basso were thrown off the tour before Landis was stripped of his tour win after failing a drug test on stage 17. Óscar Pereiro, of Spain, was handed the 2006 title.

The 2007 contenders lined up at the start of the prologue in London with more doubts swirling over cycling's credentials following the start of the Operación Puerto doping case, which centred around the drugs-in-sport network of doctor Eufemiano Fuentes.

After a tight race, it was the final time

trial that won it for Alberto Contador. The Spaniard rode a sizzling solo effort to thwart Australia's Cadel Evans, who at one point looked as if he might head into yellow before Paris. As it was, Contador won by 23 seconds.

Contador's team, Astana, felt the full force of the doping controversies the following year and were barred from entering the 2008 Tour. This paved the way for Evans to become pre-race favourite, but the Australia was once again pipped to the line by another Spaniard, this time Carlos Sastre, by 58 seconds. By this stage, Britain's Mark

Above: *Lance Armstrong (left) and Iban Mayo fall down at the end of the 15th stage, July 2003*

Cavendish had long-departed the race to prepare for the Beijing Olympics. But not before the Isle of Man sprinter opened his account with four stage wins after crashing in the opening stages the previous year. It was to mark the start of a sensational run of Tour stage wins and Cavendish still enthrals with his leg power to this day.

Cavendish racked up another six stage wins in 2009 and led home unprecedented British success. With a picture of Tom Simpson, who died on Ventoux in 1967, taped to his crossbar, Bradley Wiggins found enough resolve up the fabled climb to defend his fourth place from Andreas Kloden and Frank Schleck and thereby equal Robert Millar's all-time British best. The race was won by the returning Contador, romping to the yellow jersey by over four minutes from the gutsy Andy Schleck.

The duo returned for a memorable duel in 2010, though a winner was again to be stripped of his title after the race when the Court of Arbitration in Sport ruled against Contador following a failed doping test.

Nevertheless, it was a fierce battle on the road, culminating in semi-controversy on stage 15 when Schleck's chain popped, Contador took advantage and a mixed reception followed on the podium for the Spaniard. The Luxembourg rider took a thrilling win up the Col de Tourmalet from Contador and outdid himself on the time trial, but the Spaniard took the line honours by just under a minute.

After the Schleck-Contador duel of the previous two years, Evans came back for another assault in 2011. This time sheer determination saw him become the first Australian to win the Tour – and, at 34, also the oldest post-War winner. The key moments in a swinging battle came late on: Evans picking up time on a wet stage 16 descent to Gap and Andy Schleck gaining two minutes on the brutal Col du Galibier climb. But Evans proved unrelenting in the final time trial over the Schleck brothers (Andy and Frank finished second and third overall). Meanwhile, Cavendish became the first British winner of the points classification, thanks to a quintet of sizzling stage wins.

It set up a seismic shift in British cycling come 2012. Step forward, Wiggins, who became the first British winner of the Tour. After crashing out in 2011and breaking his collarbone, forcing him to watch proceedings on television, he became inspired by Evans' win. And

some. Before the Tour, he became the first rider in history to win Paris-Nice, Tour of Romandie and the Criterium du Dauphine. By the first mountain stage, he had claimed yellow and consolidated his position by stage 16 when he staved off a wave of attacks. All the while, teammate Chris Froome was helping Wiggins keep stable, especially on stage 17 up the Peyragudes, so much so that Britain was to end up with a one-two in Paris.

Wiggins was unable to defend his title in 2013 – an injury, as well as a well-documented clash of personalities – leaving Froome to go all out for Team Sky's second win in succession in the race's centenary year. The Briton won by over four minutes and managed to survive a treacherous last week: three Alpine stages, including a double ascent of Alpe d'Huez, as well as the determined efforts of rising star, Nairo Quintana, of Colombia, who finished second.

For the 2014 race, the rise in British cycling, coupled with the successful London Olympics, saw Yorkshire win the right to host the Grand Depart. Race organisers awarded two stages to the county in December 2012, with a third race starting from Cambridge and ending in London. The capital had previously staged the Grand Depart in the 2007 edition.

Giro d'Italia

Race Facts:
Giro d'Italia
Stage Race
UCI WorldTour
3500km
www.
girostart2014
.com

Right: *Italian cyclist Fiorenzo Magni competes in the Turin-Cannes stage of the 38th Giro Cycling Race, May 1955*

The origins of this mighty race can be traced to the rivalry between two Italian journals and an act of revenge by a bicycle manufacturer.

During the spring of 1898, having travelled by bicycle from his home in Emilia, a fresh faced 18 year old named Armando de Cougnet arrived in city of Milan. Passionate about sport, and in particular cycle racing, he was hired by the newspaper La Gazzetta dello Sport as a junior but quickly rose through the ranks to become editor of its cycling pages. Whilst conducting business in the city of Venice on 5 August 1908, de Cougnet received an urgent telegram from Tullo Morgagni, editor of La Gazzetta. "Absolutely essential for the paper you announce immediately the cycling Tour of Italy. Morgagni."

There was intrigue afoot. Morgagni had been approached by an old friend, Angelo Gatti, who once had been a senior employee with the Italian bicycle manufacturer Bianchi but had left in somewhat acrimonious circumstances following an argument with his bosses. A bicycle man through and through, Gatti quickly established his own cycle company, Atala, and took to the Bologna Cycle Show keen to sell his new machines. It was there that he met with a former colleague by the name of Tomaselli who let slip the fact that Gatti's past employer was involved in a new and special venture with the Touring Club Italiano, and the newspaper Corriere dello Sera in planning a great cycle race to rival the Tour de France. Bianchi were to oversee the cycling, Corriere dello Sport the advertising and finance and the Touring Club Italiano the race organisation drawing on the experience gained running the Giro Automobilistico. And so, Gatti had come to visit Morgagni, determined to convince the newspaperman to organise his own race and in so doing derail the plans of Bianchi and La Corriere.

It took little to convince Morgagni and the telegram to de Cougnet was despatched immediately as was a similar message to Eugene "Papa" Camillo Costamagna, the holidaying owner of La Gazzetta who was unaware of the decisions being made in his absence.

This absence was short lived. Rushing back to the newspaper's offices Costamagna convened a meeting for the very next day between himself, de Cougnet and the concerned editor. Costamagna's concern was

Above: Portrait of Alfredo Binda, many time winner of the 'Giro'

straightforward: La Gazzetta was already in financial difficulties and could ill afford the expense of a grand tour. Morgagni explained what he had learned from Gatti and pointed out that if La Corriere dello Sera's plans were to come to fruition there would be no newspaper at all.

Right: *Felice Gimondi climbing the Brocon during the 20th stage of the Giro D'Italia from Cortina - Trento.*

A plan was hatched and the very next day the front page of the Gazzetta announced the first Giro d'Italia, a race to equal the Tour de France, would be contested the following May. But it announcing a grand tour was one thing, organising and funding it was another. La Gazzetta was in an impoverished state. In later years de Cougnet recalled "It was pretty easy to announce a Giro but the realities soon hit us, because we were broke. Sometimes we didn't even have money to pay the typesetters." From somewhere 25,000 lire (about £75,000) had to be found. Although this was not a huge sum it was more that the beleaguered publication could afford.

With the assistance of an acquaintance in banking they started to raise funds. At first the process was slow but persistence bore fruit and the money started to arrive. In a clever move, rival publication La Corriere dello Sera offered 3,000 lire as first prize thus ensuring their continued association with the fledgling race. The Italian Cycling Association donated a substantial 13,900 lire with further amounts forthcoming from the San Remo Casino, Sghiria Engineering Company and other sources. The future of the race was secure.

Right: *The pack ride during the 11th stage of the Giro cycling Tour of Italy, between Marostica and Zoldo Alto, May 2005*

At precisely 2:53 in the early hours of 13 May 1909, a complement of 127 riders set off from Milan's Piazza Loreto embarking on the inaugural 2,448 kilometre Giro d'Italia. Only 49 competitors completed the eight epic stages that swept down through Bologne, Chieti, Naples and Rome then on to Florence, Genes, Turin and back to Milan.

The race was a huge success, not only capturing the imaginations of the riders but the Italian public alike who flocked to the Piazza Castello each day to read the despatches posted in the large windows of the Lancia-Lyon Peugeot dealership. Such was the fervour soldiers were called in to escort the riders in typical Italian style - on horseback and with flags flying - over the final kilometres to the finish line as 50,000 spectators looked on.

Milan Sanremo winner Luigi Gianna, appropriately riding for the Atala cycling team, became the champion of the first Giro to the delight of Atala owner Angelo Gatti whose actions had been so instrumental in the very inception of the race. For his troubles Gianna collected 5,325 lire in prize money – in comparison, Giro director Armando de Cougnet's monthly salary at the time was

150 lire.

The Italian public have a term for the best professional cyclists – Campionissimo – Champion of Champions. It is a title awarded sparingly to those few whose achievements on the bicycle are seen as almost superhuman. The first Campionissimo was Costante Girardengo, nine times Italian National Road Champion, victor of six editions of the Milan-Sanremo and Giro winner of the Giro in1919 and 1923. On his way to winning the 1919 edition he won seven of the ten stages taking the general classification by an impressive 51'52". Although at 37 seconds his overall winning margin in the 1923 edition was much smaller, Girardengo took an astonishing eight stage wins .

The 1924 edition, although won by Italian professional Giuseppe Enrici, will be forever remembered for the exploits of the 33 year old rider from Castelfranco Emilia, a village between Modena and Bologna, who finished in thirty-first place from ninety starters. This rider was farmer's daughter Alfonsina Morini Strada, the only woman ever to have competed in the Giro d'Italia alongside male competitors. This was in an age when riders were still required to

Above: *Giro d'Italia winner Ivan Basso, holds the trophy on the podium of 21th and final stage of Giro D'Italia cycling tour from Museo del Ghisallo to Milan, May 2006*

her appeal to the Italian public, all the eliminated cyclists were reinstated.

Alfonsina arrived at the finish line in Milan to the cheers of an adoring crowd. Her fame became such that she continued to live as a professional cyclist gaining some thirty career wins against male competitors. She continued to ride her bicycle for much of her life until in 1957, aged 66, she found the effort was becoming too much for her aging limbs at which point she swapped pedal-power for a red 500cc Moto-Guzzi motorcycle.

Although born in Cittiglio, Lombardy, Alfredo Binda grew up in the French city of Nice, working alongside his father from an early age for his uncle's plastering business. Regarded a talented amateur cyclist, he turned professional in 1922, aged just nineteen, but only because the Italian Cycling Federation would not issue amateur licenses to émigrés. In 1924 he accepted a contract with the Italian Legnano team. His first Giro was to be the 1925 edition. Aware that his professional team mates would not wait for him in the event of a puncture he elected to use 500 gram tyres in preference to the 390 gram tyres favoured by the top riders of the day. His foresight paid dividends and as his

conduct their own repairs, remaining totally self-sufficient, and many of the roads were unpaved and in a terrible state of repair. The shortest stage in the entire 1924 Giro was 250 kilometres. A crash on a mountain stage caused her and several male riders to finish outside the permitted time limit but, such was

LITTLE BOOK OF **CYCLE RACING**

competitors and team mates floundered on the unmade Italian roads, Binda pressed on unhindered to take overall victory by almost five minutes from Campionissimo Costante Girardengo. Remarkably he had completed the 3,520 kilometres at an average speed of 25.6 km/h without a single puncture.

Binda, whose palmares includes three World Road Championships, four Italian National Championships, three Giro di Lombardi and two Milan-Sanremo, achieved four more overall victories in the Giro d'Italia. In winning the 1927 edition he took nine of the first ten stages and two more as the race progressed. His dominance continued in 1928 with seven stage wins from a possible twelve, in 1929 as he triumphed from stage two to stage nine and then with a final victory in 1933 – a year in which he also was awarded the inaugural King of the Mountains prize as best climber. A sixth victory may have been possible had the race organisers, fearful of his domination of the race, not agreed to pay him the equivalent of the first prize, six stage wins and a bonus just to stay away. Having won a career total of 42 stages of the Giro and spent 59 days as race leader it is unsurprising that Alfredo Binda was

considered the second Campionissimo.

With Binda's reign at an end there was much speculation as to who would become the next true champion of the Giro d'Italia. In Gino Bartali their questions were in part answered as the 1935 King of the Mountains took victory first in 1936 and then again the following year. Suffering defeat in 1938 and 1939, Bartali looked to strengthen his team with the addition of a talented 20 year old who had just taken victory in the Tour of Piedmont. His name was Fausto

Below: The pack rides during the final stage of Giro D'Italia from Museo del Ghisallo to Milan, May 2006

Coppi. The Coppi-Bartali rivalry is the stuff of legend but it all started that May in 1940. Early in the race Bartali suffered a bad crash, effectively removing any chance of taking an overall victory but, impressed by his young domestique's strength and determination, he took to a supporting role and in doing so assisted Coppi in becoming the youngest ever winner of the Giro d'Italia.

Both Coppi and Bartali could have taken many more victories over the following years had it not been for the outbreak of World War Two. Coppi was drafted into the Italian army in 1942 from which he was captured during the Tunisian desert campaign of 1943. Bartali's wartime existence was somewhat different. Continuing to train he found his existence undisturbed by the fascist Italian police and occupying German troops. Unbeknownst to them, his training rides were spent first running messages for the Italian resistance movement and then later assisting Jews to escape across the border into Switzerland.

Returning to competition after the war it seemed like business as usual for the two Italian stars when, in the 1946 Giro, Bartali took victory with Coppi in second place. The following year the result would be reversed and the true rivalry would commence. Heading over the Falarego Pass, high in the Dolomites, Bartali's chain became jammed forcing him to stop. Coppi, his once faithful lieutenant, immediately attacked forcing him to chase hard but again the chain became jammed, this time causing the hapless champion to crash. A chase ensued for the next 160 kilometres as Bartali and four other riders pursued the Castellanian across the mountains. It was to no avail. Coppi won the stage by five minutes and in doing so secured his second Giro.

The fierce rivalry of these two great Italians would be their undoing in 1948. With too much time spent marking each other, countryman Fiorenzo Magni was able to secure an unpopular victory. For his trouble he was jeered and hissed all the way to Milan.

The Bartali – Coppi enmity was finally settled during the Giro of 1949. The race route had made an excursion into the French Alps with a stage that struck fear into the hearts of the peleton. Having broken away from the peleton and his rivals Coppi proceeded to ride solo across the five legendary climbs of

the Col de Madeleine, Col de Vars, Col d'Izoard, Montgenèvre and Sestrières taking victory in the Italian town of Pinerolo by a margin of over twenty minutes from second placed Bartali.

Bartali went on to take two further Giro victories in 1952 and 1953 but not before Swiss rider Hugo Koblet had become the first non-Italian in 33 editions to take victory. Koblet had started his professional cycling career as a track pursuiter but found his talents

Above: *Cycling past La torre di Pisa during the eleventh stage of the Giro d'Italia*

the slopes of the final climb the weather quickly closed in. Lashing rain first turned to sleet and hail and then to driving snow. One by one the heroes of the Giro fell by the wayside on the rough mountain roads but one man pressed on regardless of the atrocious conditions. Charly Gaul of Luxembourg, known to his fans as the Angel of the Mountains, had been languishing twenty fourth on general classification at the foot of the climb. Demolishing an already disheartened field, his solo effort over the 12 kilometre incline took him to an impressive stage win and catapulted him into first place overall, a position he defended through to the end of race to take the first of his two Giro victories – the second being three years later in 1959.

Belgian superman Eddy Merckx won his first Giro in May 1968 after attacking during a blizzard on the slopes of the Tre Cime di Lavaredo taking nine minutes from reigning champion Gimondi. His attempts for a second triumph in 1969 were undone when he was faced with allegations of drug use on the stage top Savona. Forced to leave the race against his will, the usually stoic Belgian was reduced to tears in front of a

translated well to the road – a transition that has been well repeated in more recent years by riders such as Chris Boardman, Viatcheslav Ekimov and Bradley McGee.

As the 1956 Giro headed 242 kilometres through the Dolomites from Merano to Bondone, Italian Pasquale Fornara was sitting comfortably in the maglia rosa (pink jersey). Approaching

gathered press. Constantly protesting his innocence he claimed that either he had been given a spiked drinking bottle or that his test had been tampered with and that no counter-analysis – what is now known as the B-sample – was available.

Merckx, never one to remain beaten, returned to the Giro the following year. In a demonstration of the attacking style of racing for which he had become known he took victory once again from rival Gimondi. Electing not to contest the race in 1971, Merckx took three more Giro victories in 1972, 1973 and 1974. Merckx, Ganna, Binda and Coppi remain the only four riders to have won the Giro on five occasions.

Bernard Hinault won his first Giro in 1980 after breaking clear on the hallowed climb of the Stelvio, at 2,757 metres the highest mountain pass in Italy, with Renault team-mate Jean-René Bernardeau. Returning to the race in 1982 Hinault found himself a marked man as an unofficial coalition of Italian teams fought to combat his dominance. Their efforts were to no avail as once again the Badger monopolised proceedings to take his second victory with a margin of 2'35" over Swedish Bianchi leader Tommy Prim. Hinault's

third and final Giro outing was in 1984. Having won the 1983 edition, Francesco Moser was favoured to take victory but found himself with a 1'15" deficit going into the final time-trial. The reigning hour record holder rode well but was able to close only seven seconds on the determined Frenchman who was forced to ride the entire stage bombarded by the taunts and jeers of a partisan crowd before taking his third Giro win.

Controversy reared its familiar head

Below: *Italian rider Mario Cipollini pedals during the 87th Giro between Porreta Terme and Civitella in Val di Chiana*

in 1987. The Carrera team was jointly led by Italian Roberto Visentini, winner of the 1986 race, and Irishman Stephen Roche, who had already won the Tour of Valencia and Tour de Romandie in addition to placing fourth in the Paris-Nice and second in Liège-Bastogne-Liège. The two riders had an agreement that they would work together for the good of the team until one of them was able to take a commanding lead, at which point the other would ride in a supporting role. All went well for the first two weeks with both riders taking a share in the lead until Visentini took control following the individual time-trial. However, Roche's pursuit of an escaping rider with Scotland's Robert Millar and the remaining overall contenders was met with protestation from his team. Ordered to wait for Visentini, Roche disobeyed, choosing instead to ride his own race. By the send of the stage the Irishman was back in Pink with his Visentini pushed back to seventh place 3'12" in arrears.

With the exception of long term friend and domestique Eddy Schepers, Roche's Italian teammates refused to support him for the remainder of the race but he soon found new allies in Millar and Australian Phil Anderson, both of whom had ridden with the Dubliner for the famous Paris based amateur club ACBB, and the Belgian Panasonic squad who were happy to see Visentini relegated down the leader board. Roche triumphed with a margin of almost four minutes from ally Robert

Miguel Induráin, first in 1992 and then again in 1993. An attempted hat-trick in 1994 was foiled by the efforts of Russian second-year professional Evgeni Berzin riding for the Gewiss squad. Second place was taken by a young Marco Pantani following two solo mountain top stage wins that announced to the world his arrival as one of the best riders of his generation. Always a popular rider, the public were shocked when he was involved in a serious collision with a Jeep on a descent of the Pino Torinese during the Milan Torino. The impact shattered his left leg leaving his future as a professional cyclist in serioud doubt.

Pantani, known to his fans as the Pirate, reemerged at the 1997 Giro but his planned return to greatness was thwarted when a black cat ran out in front of him whilst descending into Chiunzi, causing him to crash and forcing his retirement from the race. The 1998 season was to be Pantani's greatest. His win over Pavel Tonkov and Alex Zülle in the Giro acted as a precursor to a dominating performance in a troubled Tour de France.

However, Pantani's fortunes took a turn for the worse. He started the 1999 Giro d'Italia as a clear favorite and in

Millar before going on to record wins in the Tour de France and World Road Race Championship in the same year to become only the second rider, after Eddy Merckx, to take the hallowed Triple-Crown of cycling.

The 1990s produced two notable victories for Tour de France legend

taking a solo win on stage eight had been propelled into the pink jersey. Three more dominant stage wins at Oropa, Alpe de Pampeagno and Madonna di Campaglio followed and with just two stages remaining he held five and a half minute lead over compatriot Ivan Gotti. Then, in a random test, it was discovered that he had a suspiciously high haematocrit (red blood cell) count which suggested, although did not prove, the use of Erythropoietin (EPO). Athough he constantly protested his innocence, Pantani was banished from the race leaving the door wide open for Gotti to take a second Giro victory following his triumph in 1997.

Moving into the new millennium, Italian dominance has once again reigned supreme. Stefano Garzelli had been employed by his Mercatone Uno team to act as super-domestique for Marco Pantani but in 2000, with the Pirate lacking form, he was relieved of team duties and offered the chance to fight his own Giro battle, assisted by the Pirate himself. Always in contention, it a was a strong performance in the final time trial that allowed Garzelli to take the pink jersey away from race leader Francesco Casagrande who was struggling with an inflamed sciatic nerve. In true style Garzelli dedicated his victory to his one-time mentor Pantani.

Gilberto Simoni may have won the 2003 edition but it will always be remembered as Mario Cipollini's Giro. Loved by the Italian public for his overt displays of showmanship "The Lion King" had always talked a big game and then delivered in style. He would frequently taunt the UCI by competing in specially designed skin-suits and jerseys in contravention of the rules. The thousands of Swiss francs paid in subsequent fines bestowed yet more welcome publicity. However, his record of Giro d'Italia stage wins proved that his ability was well in proportion to his flamboyancy. Alfredo Binda's record of 41 Giro stage wins had seemed insurmountable but, in 2003, on the 160 kilometre ninth stage from Arezzo to Montecatini, Cipollini, resplendent in his rainbow jersey as reigning World Champion, outsprinted Australian Robbie McEwen to take his forty second stage victory.

The 2006 Giro d'Italia was completely dominated by just one rider, Ivan Basso. The tall, slender Italian won three of the six mountain stages and the team time trial with his CSC team-mates in what was considered the toughest Giro route for many years. His winning margin of 9'18" was the largest since Adorni Vittorio triumphed over Italo Zilioli in 1965.

In recent years, Russian Denis Menchov broke dreams of a home victory by winning the centenary edition in 2009, while the lead changed hands eight times the following year as Spain's Basso secured his second crown. Alberto Contador has also triumphed, but, tainted by drug accusations, saw his 2010 title and results since that race scrapped by CAS.

For the 2014 race, organisers revealed a route that would take the race outside of continental Europe for the first time. The Grande Partenza would take place over three days across both sides of the border in Ireland. It would involve routes in Belfast, around the stunning Causeway Coast and Armagh before moving on to Dublin.

The Tour de France may be seen as the biggest cycle race in the world but it is the Giro d'Italia that is the most passionate. With Ireland staging races, that passion to connect has continued too.

Below: *The 19th stage of the Giro*

Vuelta Españia

Race Facts:

Stage Race
UCI WorldTour
3400km
www.lavuelta.
com

Opposite:
*A Spanish
propaganda
poster from the
Spanish Civil War,
with an illustration
of armed soldiers
and barbed wire
and the words,
'Defending Madrid
is Defending
Catalonia'*

For a number of years Spain had been the home of two tours of reasonable international standing. The Tour of Catalunya had established itself well on the professional calendar since its first edition in 1911 and although much younger the Tour of the Basque Country had already attracted riders in great numbers from across Europe and was not won by a Spaniard until Mariano Cañardo's triumphant 1930 victory. There was though little interest in promoting a national tour of any description.

Spain, although similar in size, boasted a population of only two thirds that of its neighbour France. It was a nation of great contrast from its factory filled industrialised north that had embraced the new wave of European consumerism to the pastoral and somewhat primitive south whose roots were still firmly set in another century. The country had also experienced many years of political upheaval. Its army had suffered terrible losses in Morocco at the hands of Abd el-Krim and his Riffi forces and then, in September 1923, Miguel Primo de Rivera had seized power in a military coup throwing the nation into a dictatorship that would last until his death in 1930, the subsequent abdication of King Alfonso XIII and the formation in 1931 of the Second Spanish Republic.

It is true though, that the greatest cycle races have all been started by the dreams and visions of a committed individual. In the case of the Vuelta a España this individual was a retired cyclist by the name of Clemente López Dóriga whose inauspicious racing career had in no way detracted from his passion for cycle sport. Inspired by the grand tours of France and Italy, López Dóriga approached the Spanish press, resolute that Spain should have its own national tour but was met with indifference and argument.

However, López Dóriga's fortunes changed when he was introduced to Juan Pujol, director of the Madrid based daily newspaper Informaciones, a man who shared his characteristic drive and determination. Pujol's enthusiasm was certainly driven by his desire to increase the circulation and profile of his publication but he was also a patriot and looked on the Vuelta as an opportunity to unite a nation torn by years of disquiet.

And so, in February 1935, the Vuelta Ciclista a España was announced in the pages of Informaciones – astonishingly to be held at the end of April that very year. Invitations were quickly sent out to Europe's best teams and rider but many were greeted with a feeling of scepticism. Was it really possible that this inexperienced newspaperman could

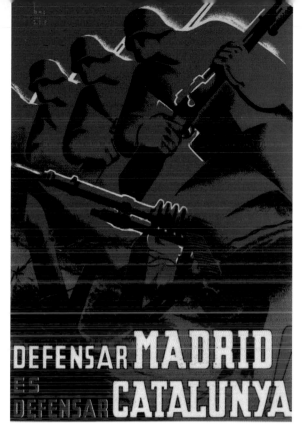

organise such a major race in little more than two months? Furthermore the race was planned to conclude just four days before the opening stage of the Giro d'Italia so many riders were already committed to ride the established race.

It was, therefore, to the amazement of

Above: *Sean Kelly in action*

in the heart of Madrid to embark on the inaugural twelve stage, 3,425 kilometre Vuelta a España.

The opening stage set a tone of excitement that would stay with the Vuelta to this day. After just 90 kilometres of racing Belgian Antoon Digneff and Spaniard Mariano Cañardo, winner of both the Tour of Catalunya and the Tour of the Basque Country, broke clear of the peleton. For the next 95 kilometres the two riders stayed clear, although it was Cañardo who was seen to do most of the work. Approaching the finish in the town of Valladolid it seemed likely that the first Vuelta stage win would be taken by a home rider – Cañardo's ability to sprint had assisted his Catalan and Basque wins – but, just metres from the line, his front wheel dropped into a tram line on the cobbled street. Struggling to stay upright, Cañardo narrowly avoided a crash but his momentum was lost, as was the stage when Digneff cruised past to take the win.

The 1935 Vuelta was ultimately won by another Belgian, twenty-one year old Gustave Deloor, who had taken control of the race following the third stage into Bilbao. As consolation for his first stage misfortune, Cañardo finished second on

many observers that on the morning of 29 April 1935, thirty and two Spaniards, six Belgians, four Italians, two French, two Swiss, two Dutch and two Austrians cycled away from the Puerta de Atocha the 29 survivors having previously won the fifth stage from San Sebastián to Zaragoza.

Accompanied on the podium by his elder brother Alphonse, who had taken second place, and Italian Antonio Bertola, Gustave Deloor triumphed once more as the Vuelta returned for its second edition in the spring of 1936. The hopes of a Spanish victory had been dashed early in the race in part by in-fighting between riders but also because of a serious bout of bad luck on the second stage which saw a multitude of punctures, the felling of two riders by a stray mule and a collision between Mariano Cañardo's bicycle and a dog.

Six weeks after the end of the 1936 Vuelta the Iberian political climate changed dramatically and the nation descended into a vicious Civil War that ultimately would cost half a million lives.

In 1941 the Vuelta returned with the support the Gol newspaper and the National Ministry of Education and Leisure with General Franco's ruling nationalist government keen to divert public attention from ongoing internal difficulties. Thirty two riders readied themselves for the start outside the Ministry offices in Madrid's Puerta

del Sol where, arms raised in salute, they sang Cara al Sol, the anthem of the fascist Falange party. The winner in both 1941 and 1942 was Spaniard Julian Berrendero, a former Tour de France stage winner and of King of the Mountains who, as a republican, had spent the course of the Civil War living and racing in France with many other Spanish riders. On returning to his homeland in 1939 he was arrested, possibly for anti-Franco comments made

Below: *Spain Iles Balears cycling team's Alejandro Valverde crosses the finish line to win the Tour of the Basque Country vuelta al Pais Vasco fourth stage, a 167 km run between Vitoria and Alsasua, northern Spain, 2005*

some three years before, and imprisoned in a succession of concentration camps.

Despite the lack of Spanish involvement, the Vuelta disappeared again from the calendar in 1943 and 1944 as war continued to rage across much of Europe. Three days after the cessation of European conflict, on 10 May 1945, the fifth Vuelta commenced albeit with a peleton consisting entirely of Iberian contenders. Fifty-one riders contested the nineteen stages – forty three Spaniards and eight Portuguese – over almost 3,800 kilometres of the toughest of roads. Despite taking three road stages, former champion Berrendero was beaten to the overall victory by Delio Rodriguez of the Galindo team.

As the years passed, the Vuelta struggled on despite forced cancellations in 1949 and again for four years between 1951 and 1954 due to financial difficulties. Spain was still suffering from the Civil War and had been politically ostracised, refused foreign aid and subjected to a trade embargo.

With much needed financial assistance forthcoming from the United States in return for allowing the presence of US military bases, Spain was, by 1955, starting to recover from its monetary woes and the so called Años de Hambre – the Years of Hunger. It was at this time that Alejandro Echevarría, director of the Basque newspaper El Correo Español-El Pueblo Vasco made a decision to revive the Vuelta once more, injecting a colossal six million pesetas.

For the first time the Vuelta was able to boast a truly international field. The 106 rider field included twelve man

teams from France and Italy, six man teams from Switzerland and Britain and two riders from Germany. The route itself, at 2,740 kilometres was far shorter than in previous editions with just fifteen stages to test the riders. As was the custom in the Tour de France, Vuelta riders were required to ride for their nation rather than their professional team. The sixty Spanish contenders were split into two national and eight regional teams, a strategy that forced together two of the country's greatest rivals; Frederico Bahamontes and Jesús Loroño. More differing characters would be impossible to find. Bahamontes, the Eagle of Toledo, was gregarious but unpredictable whereas Loroño, the Larrabetzu Lion, was a quiet, calculating character.

The first regenerated tour commenced

at 11:48 on the morning of 23 April 1955 in the Basque city of Bilbao to the cheers of an enormous gathered crowd. Unusually for a grand tour, the race headed straight into the mountains producing, perhaps intentionally, an ideal chance for the home-nation riders to shine in front of their fiercely partisan fans. But it became apparent that things would not go to plan as French climber Gilbert Bauvin stole away from the peleton on the slopes of the Azcarate to cross the finish line in San Sebastián with a 1'18" advantage to take the amarillo Jersey.

Determined to recover their losses, Bahamontes and Loroño attacked on the next stage as the peleton climbed the Jaizkibel, a first category climb that still features in the San Sebastian Classic. However, with the stage scheduled to finish in Bayonne, a city geographically in France but still part of the Basque region, the French protagonists were not prepared to stand by and watch their Iberian rivals pedal away. Bauvin and compatriot Louis Bergaud crossed the gap and, to the further frustration of the Spaniards, Bauvin rode ahead to take his second stage win. The following day, with Bauvin unable to repeat his success, the amarillo jersey passed to

Loroño. But, as the race progressed, internal squabbling within and between the Spanish squads reared its head. On the stage to Lerida a group of French riders broke clear, gaining a 12 minute advantage on Loroño. Three members of the Spanish team were also ahead having tried to hunt down the break whilst the remaining two, including Bahamontes were exhausted after chasing the peleton following a puncture. Loroño had no choice other than to pursue on his own but it was to no avail, as the leader's jersey was lost to Raphaël Géminiani. When the final stage returned to Bilbao it was another Frenchman, Jean Dotto, who was in yellow having gained over twenty minutes on the peleton in just two stages.

Word soon spread of the successful new Vuelta and as each year passed the quality of the field improved, also perhaps influenced by the generous incentives paid to the top riders. The 1956 edition was graced by the presence of three time Tour winner Louison Bobet and Swiss star Hugo Koblet, winner of the Giro, the Tour and the World Championship. However, it was Italian Angelo Conterno who took victory having seized the amarillo jersey

on the second stage from Albacete and Alicante and successfully defending his lead all the way to Bilbao. Once again, any hope of a Spanish success was dashed by recurring discord within the team despite the presence of newly appointed directeur sportif Luis Puig.

The 1957 Vuelta was to be different. International interest was supplied by all three podium finishers of the previous year's Tour de France and Gastone Nencini who, within six weeks, would be crowned champion of the fortieth Giro d'Italia. Friction still existed in the Spanish team but at last Puig seemed to have the better of the situation. The rule was simple – whichever rider was best placed of general classification would be team leader.

Consistent riding in the first two stages had rewarded Loroño with third place on classification but, early in the action on stage three, Bahamontes had slipped away with thirteen riders. On the final climb of the day the Eagle of Toledo flew solo from the break, ultimately finishing the stage with a fourteen minute advantage on the peleton to don the amarillo jersey for the first time in his racing career. The following day Loroño, livid with his so-

Opposite:
France's Cofidis cycling team's David Moncoutie crosses the finish line 05 April 2005, to win the second stage of the Tour of the Basque Country-Vuelta al Pais Vasco, a 166 km run between Zarautz and Trapagaran, northern Spain

Right: Spain's Joaquin Rodriguez (centre) of Saunier Duval Team rides during the sixth stage of the Tour of Spain

called team mate's action, attacked early, determined to make the Basque pay, but for once the weather played its part as heavy snowfalls brought the stage to a premature close.

Loroño's opportunity for retribution came on the 192 kilometre tenth stage from Valencia to the Catalonian town of Tortosa. Bernardo Ruiz, leader of the Spanish regional Mediterranean team, was no fan of Bahamontes. Signaling to Loroño to follow he instigated a fierce attack from which a small break emerged. Bahamontes suddenly realised his lead

was in danger and tried desperately to react but team boss Luis Puig blocked the way with his car whilst team mates Cosme Barrutia and Jesús Galdeano held onto his clothing leaving him helpless as the Loroño / Ruiz train finished the stage with a 22 minute advantage. The amarillo jersey had changed owner once again and at last Loroño was in a commanding lead.

For the remainder of the race, with his hopes of an overall victory dashed, Bahamontes concentrated his efforts on the King of the Mountains. His efforts

not only won him that coveted title but also went second place in the general classification. Finally the ecstatic crowds were treated not only to a Spanish victory but to an all Spanish podium, with the third step occupied by Loroño's stage ten ally Ruiz.

With the national team format consigned to the history books since a change of regulations in 1959, the crack Helyett-St Raphaël professional team arrived at the 1962 Vuelta with a single intention. Their team leader, French national hero Jacques Anquetil,

already possessed two Tour de France victories and the honour of being the first Frenchman to win the Giro d'Italia. It was his desire to become the first rider in history to win all three major tours.

The St Raphael squad dominated the race from the outset. By the end of the first week they had won the team time trial and three individual stages placing Germany's Rudi Altig, the reigning World Pursuit Champion, in the amarillo jersey with team-mate Seamus Elliott of Ireland in a close second place. All went well for Altig until the ninth

Above: *Spain's Roberto Heras celebrates after winning the Tour of Spain, La Vuelta, cycling race in September 2005 in Madrid*

Altig in a stunning demonstration of that put the German back into the amarillo jersey. Anquetil left the race in disgust the very next day leaving the selfless Elliott to defend Altig's lead all the way to Bilbao.

Anquetil returned the following year and, with no intention of making the same mistake twice, had ensured Altig was not included on the team preferring the support of the loyal Elliot and World Champion Jean Stablinski. Anquetil stamped his authority on the race the very first day by winning the 52 kilometre time-trial with an astonishing 2'51" margin. Once again the Helyett-St Raphaël squad policed the race and despite constant attacks no rider could unseat the Frenchman who went on to win with a margin of 3'06" from Spaniard Colmenarejo

stage when, having punctured, he failed to receive a wheel from any of his team. At the end of the stage Elliot was now race leader. As the race progressed Elliott successfully marked each break but, with his team-leader expected to do well in the final time-trial, he loyally refused to make any gain. However, Anquetil's anticipated domination of the stage 15 time-trial did not go to plan as he was unexpectedly beaten by his team-mate

For many years the organisers of the Vuelta had tried in vain to secure the attendance of the great Eddy Merckx. On each occasion their request had been denied, not for of a lack of interest from the rider himself, but because his sponsors, Molteni, had no commercial interests in Spain and considered their two wheeled super-advert best placed elsewhere. But at last, in 1973, he agreed. With four

Tour de France victories already under his belt, not to mention three Giros, two World Championships, a bevy of classics and the Hour Record, the prospect of Merckx dominating yet another Grand Tour caught the imagination of the press and the public across Europe.

Merckx took the prologue time-trial with ease and felt untroubled in loosing the amarillo jersey to Dutch sprinter Gerben Karstens on the third stage. His dominating Molteni squad was as well drilled as Anquetil's Raphaël guard had been some ten years earlier. As often happens in professional racing, things didn't go wholly to plan. On the hilly fourth stage from Alcazar de San Juan to Cuenca, Kas team leader José Pesarronda slipped clear of the peleton accompanied only by Molteni's Jos Deschoenmaecker. Merckx sat comfortably in the peleton, aware that Deschoenmaecker would do no work and that the absconding Spaniard could be reeled back in at will. But, with just fifteen kilometres remaining on the stage, news broke that the gap to the escapees was four minutes and not one as had been reported by race radio. The Molteni squad chased hard, recovering two of the lost minutes, but, despite Deschoenmaecker comfortably taking

the stage win, Pesarronda had stolen the amarillo jersey from Merckx's back.

The following day, with a gap of 1'25" to recover, Molteni once again took control of the race. Absent from many of the intermediate sprints to conserve energy, Merckx burst forth in the closing metres of the stage only

Above:
Alessandro
Petacchi of Italy
celebrates on
the podium after
winning the last
stage of the Tour of
Spain, La Vuelta,
cycling race in
September, 2005

Right: *Alejandro Valverde (right) of Illes Balears cycling team crosses the finish line to win the first stage of the Tour of the Basque Country - Vuelta al Pais Vasco cycling race, 03 April 2006*

to be beaten on the line by compatriot Eddy Peelman of the Rokado team who, assisted by a hand-sling from a team mate, had rocketed almost from nowhere to take victory. However, incensed by his apparent thievery, the Molteni team registered a protest which was duly upheld and the stage was awarded to Merckx. For the remainder of the Vuelta, the Molteni squad closed ranks making an attack on Merckx all but impossible. His imminent victory was underlined by a definitive victory in the 17.5 kilometre final time trial which saw second placed Pesarronda finish 53 seconds adrift.

The mid-seventies were years of change for Spain and the Vuelta. Franco's death in 1975 had signaled a new beginning for the country but the transition was not to be easy. Throughout the years of dictatorship the race had often started and finished in the Basque Country as a reminder to its inhabitants and the world that the region was part of the Spain. The Basque separatist organisation ETA was involved in a terrorist campaign that was shaking the whole country.

A mere 70 competitors started the 1977 Vuelta as fears safety fears combined

with an airline strike kept riders away. It did, though, feature one of the biggest names in cycling – the Belgian sprinter Freddy Maertens – who had taken eight stages of the Tour de France the previous

once seriously challenged for the overall classification. Claiming a phenomenal thirteen out of nineteen stages victory for the Belgian was never in doubt.

The 1978 Vuelta will always be remembered, but unfortunately for the wrong reasons. The penultimate stage was disrupted when, after 50 kilometres, the peleton entered Durango to find the road barricaded by Basque separatists who had covered the tarmac with tacks, rocks and pieces of timber. The entire field was subsequently bussed to Zarauz to ride the remaining 34 kilometres to San Sebastián. With the following day's final time trial prematurely abandoned after riders were subjected to taunts and missiles, Bernard Hinault was declared winner of the Vuelta, the podium positions having remained unchanged since the twelfth stage.

With these actions the future of the Vuelta looked in trouble. In January of 1979, El Correo Español-El Pueblo Vasco, organiser of the Vuelta since 1955, withdrew its support sighting financial difficulties. The cancellation of Spain's grand tour was announced. It was at this time that Luis Puig, by now President of the Spanish Cycling Federation, became involved. Returning from Italy,

year. After collecting the naranja jersey at the prologue time trial - the traditional yellow, or amarillo, jersey having been relegated to the sidelines in favour of an orange one – Maertens was never

Above: The pack rides during the sixth stage of the Tour of Spain from Cuenca to Valdelinares, 01 September 2005

he immediately enlisted the support of Unipublic, a business solely involved in the promotion of sporting events, and the clothing company Lois as prime sponsor. The Vuelta a España had once again been saved.

Hinault returned to the Vuelta once again in 1983 confident of collecting a second victory in the race. Many expected the French Tour hero to dominate from start to finish in the same manner as had been seen with Maertens in 1977 but there was a new breed of rider on the block determined not to

jersey and his second Vuelta during the seventeenth stage in a masterful attack on the slopes of the Puerto de Serranillos.

The prologue time-trial of the 1985 Vuelta brought a new name into the cycling limelight. Bert Ooserbosch, leader of the Panasonic team, had lived up to anticipation by taking victory on the 5.6 kilometre Valladolid course, less predicted was the impressive second place ride of a young Reynolds team domestique named Miguel Indurain. The Spaniard's arrival on the professional scene was affirmed the following day when, after placing well on the stage behind winning sprinter Eddy Planckaert, he unexpectedly found himself the wearer of the amarillo jersey. Indurain defended the jersey well until the stage six ascent of the Covadonga where an in form Pedro Delgado took over control. But Delgado's fortune was short lived. The next day, overcome by his efforts on the Covadonga he cracked and the leader's jersey first passed to the shoulders of his team mate Pello Ruiz Cabestany and then three days later to those of Peugeot team leader Robert Millar of Scotland.

Seven days later, following an eventful time trial stage, Millar was still

let the old hand have it all his own way. The expected clash with Italian World Road Champion Guiseppe Saronni was not forthcoming – he had already stated his intentions for the Giro – but Hinault was pushed hard all the way, finally staking his claim to the amarillo

Above: Spain's Roberto Heras (right) chats with Isidro Nozal before the 21th and final stage of the Vuelta, the Tour of Spain, 2003

in yellow with just two stages remaining – ten seconds clear of Columbian Pacho Rodríguez and 1'15" ahead of Spaniard Ruiz Cabestany. With the Scot marking any attempt they made, it became apparent to Ruiz Cabestany and Rodríguez that attacking Millar on the penultimate stage was impossible. Seemingly unable to threaten the general classification, little interest was shown when Kelme rider José Recio disappeared up the road in search of a stage win and not much more attention

was paid when Ruiz Cabestany's team-mate, Pedro Delgado, followed suit. After a short chase the two riders made contact and with the encouragement of the Kelme directeur sportif the two escapees made good work gradually extending their lead.

Millar, convinced he had won the Vuelta outright, was making light of the stage by chatting to other riders and offering his commiserations to those who had come so close. It was then that his race would explode as world reached him of the break. Delgado had started the stage six minutes in deficit but was now in a break five minutes ahead with only 40 kilometres left to race. Looking around Millar had an awful realisation that there was not a single Peugeot team-mate in sight. As the peleton crossed the line 6'50" in arrears Millar's hopes of victory vanished.

Irishman Sean Kelly had always been a popular rider to the Spanish public and his 1988 victory was met with delight. It was seen in many ways as suitable compensation for the woes of his ride the previous year. Having won a stage he was leading the race just three days from the finish when he was forced to have a painful saddle sore removed by surgery. The following day, just 14 kilometres into the stage, the wound became inflamed forcing him to abandon and leaving Columbian Luis Herrera to take victory.

The 1992 Vuelta developed into a thrilling three way tussle between Switzerland's Tony Rominger and Spain's Jesús Montoya and Pedro Delgado. Rominger finally took his grip on the race with an awe inspiring ride in the stage 19 time-trial but his efforts had been well assisted some ten stages earlier on the ascent of the Tourmalet. As the three climbed together Montoya's Amaya team manager repeatedly shouted instruction to stick to Delgado's wheel no matter what. In response Delgado slowed, eventually coming to a complete halt – Montoya unsure what to do followed suit allowing the amused Swiss to ride away and into contention. Tony Rominger repeated his winning form in 1993 and 1994 to become the first rider to win three editions of the Vuelta.

In 1995 the Vuelta underwent a major change as the race was moved from its traditional April slot on the professional calendar to September. Distanced from the Giro and seen as a second opportunity for Tour de France

riders the race took on a new lease of life and has thrived on its increased profile. Swiss success continued in 1996 as Alex Zülle took victory accompanied on the rostrum by compatriots Laurent Dufaux and Rominger. The remainder of the decade saw a second triumph for Zülle and wins for Spain's Abraham Olano and German powerhouse Jan Ullrich. 1999 saw the introduction of the hardest climb in professional road racing the 12.55 kilomere ascent of the Alto de El Angliru which at its steepest has a gradient of

Above: Spain's Roberto Heras rides during the 21th and final stage of the Vuelta, the Tour of Spain, 28 September 2003 between Madrid and Madrid

23.6% (almost 1 in 4).

The new millennium saw a return to Spanish dominance of the Vuelta with wins for Roberto Heras in 2000, Angel Luis Casero in 2001 at a record average speed of 42.16 km/h and for Aitor González in 2002.

Roberto Heras achieved two more Vuelta wins in 2003 and 2004 to become only the second rider in history to win the Vuelta on three occasions. In 2005 he attempted to go one better with a fourth triumph and after a hard fought race was initially crowned victor. He was stripped of his title two months later after testing positive for EPO.

The 2011 race proved a highly-significant tour result as Chris Froome and Bradley Wiggins, who finished second and third, became the first British riders to finish on the podium of a grand tour since 1987.

The 2013 race proved a quite astonishing one when American veteran Chris Horner won the race in Madrid at the tender age of 41 to become the oldest Grand Tour winner. In over 250 editions of the big three, no man over the age of 36, since Belgian Firmin Lambot won the 1922 Tour de France, had previously triumphed.

Paris – Nice

Race Facts:
Stage Race
UCI WorldTour
1300km
www.letour.fr

Right: Bradley Wiggins in 2012

Paris – Nice, The Race to the Sun, is the first UCI WorldTour event of the year featuring in the second week of March. A creation of Albert Lejeune, director of le Petit Journal, the inaugural race started at the Place d'Italie in the heart of Paris on 14 March 1933 to be won by Belgian Alfons Schepers.

Seen as the traditional season pipe-opener, the race bears southwest through the heart of France, climbing over the Alps before heading to the Côte d'Azur to finish on the Promenades des Anglais in Nice. The race is rated HC, Hors Categorie, by the UCI placing it just one step down from the Grand Tours of France, Italy and Spain.

Two riders have dominated the history of the Race to the Sun. Jacques Anquetil achieved five Paris-Nice wins between 1957 and 1966 culminating in an historic showdown with Raymond Poulidor which saw him take victory by just 48 seconds after attacking on the final stage. This achievement pails into insignificance when compared to the astounding performance of Ireland's Sean Kelly who won on seven consecutive occasions between 1982 and 1988. Bradley Wiggins won in 2012, the same year as his Tour de France success.

Tirreno – Adriatico

Running concurrently with the Paris-Nice and considered equally important as preparation for the Milan-Remo one day classic, the Hor Categorie rated Tirreno – Adriatico is the first major stage race of the Italian professional road-racing calendar. Organised by Gazzetta dello Sport, the Italian newspaper responsible for the Giro d'Italia, the race crosses Italy west to east from the Mediterranean to finish in San Benedetto del Tronto on the Adriatic coast, the competition has become known as the Race of the Two Seas.

Since Italian Dino Zandegu claimed victory in the inaugural 1966 edition, the race has doubled in distance from approximately 600 to 1200 kilometres increasing from three stages to seven.

Belgium ace Roger de Vlaeminck regularly used the Tirreno – Adriatico as training for the Spring Classics. Between 1972 and 1977 he was untouchable, winning the race on six occasions and collecting fifteen stage wins.

The race has, since 2005, taken on a new lease of life having been included as an integral part of, first the UCI ProTour, then the WorldTour.

Race Facts:

Stage Race
UCI WorldTour
1100km
www.gazzetta.
it/Speciali/
TirrenoAdriatico/
en

Left: *The peloton rides on the seafront of the seventh stage of the Tirreno-Adriatico race, March 2006*

Milan – Sanremo

Race Facts:
1 Day Race
 UCI WorldTour
294km
www.
milansanremo.
co.uk

The brainchild of Eugenio Costamagna, editor of the Italian newspaper La Gazzetta dello Sport, the 294 kilometre Milan – Sanremo is the longest of the one-day classics. Following a tough route from the Lombardy plains over the Apennines to the Ligurian coast the race is dominated by the climbs of the Turchino Pass, the Cipressa and the Poggio.

The inaugural edition was first run in April 1907. After 100 kilometres of racing Italian favourite Giovanni Gerbi, taking advantage of local knowledge and poor weather conditions, attacked at the town of Pozzolo Formigaro pursued only by French rider Gustave Garrigou. Reaching the port of Savona the battling pair was joined by Gerbi's Bianchi team mate, the great Lucien Petit-Breton. On the approach to Sanremo the Italian grabbed hold of a surprised Garrigou allowing Petit Breton to ride away to victory. Despite beating Garrigou in the sprint for second place Gerbi was relegated to third following a complaint for irregular riding. The fourth placed rider took another thirty minutes to cross the line.

The 1910 edition of the race was fought in the most atrocious of conditions. Eugène Christophe, famous for repairing his broken forks during the 1913 Tour, reached the summit of the Turchino pass on foot through driving snow. Descending into the valley he passed his competitors one by one as they

abandoned but conditions worsened. Standing against a rock at the side of the road he found himself unable to move as the signs of exposure to effect. A passing local Italian dragged him into a small inn where he sat by a fire and drank rum to get warm. Twenty five minutes later, supplied with a pair of long trousers, Christophe set out into the cold and pressed on, passing the remaining riders to take a famous win after an ordeal lasting almost twelve and a half hours. The second placed rider, Luigi Ganna finished seventy minutes later. Of the 63 riders who started in Milan only four reached Sanremo.

During the early years of the race Italian Campionissimo Costante Girardengo dominated the race, winning six times from 1918 to 1928. Cycling's greatest rivals, Gino Bartali and Fausto Coppi, achieved seven wins between them starting in 1939 and culminating in 1950. The greatest rider of "La Primavera", as the race is often known, was undoubtedly the Cannibal himself, Eddy Merckx who won the event seven times between 1966 and 1976. In more recent years the most dominant rider has been German sprinter Erik Zabel, winner four times between 1997 and 2001. Mark Cavendish sprinted to victory in 2009, becoming only the second Briton to win since Tom Simpson in 1964.

Above: *Cyclists pass close to the sea during the 96th Milan - San Remo Classic*

Tour of Flanders

Race Facts:
1 Day Race
UCI WorldTour
250km
www.rondevan
vlaanderen.be

The Tour of Flanders, know locally as De Ronde, was the creation of Belgian journalist and cycling fan Karel van Wynendaele. When invited to assist in the creation of the "Sportwereld" newspaper he immediately saw an opportunity to organise a bicycle race in the mould of the Paris-Roubaix. The inaugural event of 1912 was far from a success with only 37 riders taking part over a 330 kilometre loop which culminated in four laps of a wooden track around a pond in Mariakerke, Gent. With the onset of the First World War in 1914 the outlook for this fledgling race looked dim.

The earliest editions of the Ronde took place two weeks before Easter, often clashing with the Milan-San Remo precluding the attendance of the top Italian and French riders. In 1948 with the foundation of the Challenge Desgrange-Colombo, a forerunner to the UCI World Cup and in turn the ProTour the race was moved back seven days, appearing one week before the great Paris-Roubaix. At last the best riders arrived and the future of the race was secured thanks to the dedication of its organiser.

Like so many of the spring classics the Tour of Flanders is inextricably linked with the weather. Perhaps the greatest Ronde victory was that of Eddy Merckx in 1969. Despite an impressive palmarès the press of the day

cast doubt over his ability to win the race. In freezing conditions and gale force winds Merckx, determined to prove a point, set about demolishing the field. With 64 kilometers to go to the finish, realizing that the best riders were struggling to make the pace, he rode off the front of the field leaving all in his wake. Upon crossing the finish line he was to wait a further five minutes before catching sight of second placed Felice Gimondi. It is little wonder that the great Eddy Merckx was known as The Cannibal.

Until 2011, the race started in Bruges and headed west to Oostende before sweeping southeast into the heart of Flanders. From 2011, the race finished in Oudenaarde. After 145 kilometres of riding competitors reach the Molenberg first of a series of 17 climbs that will occupy their next 100 kilometres of racing. Names like the Kwaremont, Muur, Bosberg and Valkenberg are as much part of cycling history as Merckx, Bartali or Hinault.

Gent – Wevelgem

Race Facts:
1 Day Race
UCI World Tour
210km
www.gent-
wevelgem.be

The first Gent – Wevelgem was organised in the September of 1934 by Belgian enthusiasts Leon Baekelandt, Gerard Margodt and Georges Matthijs as a tribute to the great Gaston Rebry, a resident of Wevelgem who had won both the Ronde van Vlaanderen (Tour of Flanders) and the Paris-Roubaix. Originally a race of 120 kilometres for junior riders, the field was opened to independents, or semi-professionals, in 1936 taking on full professional status from its first post war edition in July 1945 when Belgian Robert van Eenaeme took victory from compatriot Maurice van Herzele.

Over its many years Gent – Wevelgem has attracted a strong international field but for many years the results were dominated by homebred riders. French cycling legend Jacques Anquetil scored a famous victory in 1964 after jumping clear of a surprised bunch with just two miles to go. A ferocious chase erupted with the peleton gradually closing down on the lone breakaway. Anquetil fought back, hanging on to his slim lead as if his life depended on it until he jubilantly crossed the finish line just one second ahead of the fast moving Belgian sprinters.

British rider Barry Hoban of the Gan-Mercier team took victory in the 1974 race in a bunch sprint with Eddy Merckx and Roger de Vlaeminck. Lizzie Armitstead won the inaugural women's race in 2012.

In its current form the race follows a tough route across the lanes of Belgium 55 kilometres west from the town of Deinze to Oostende and then southwest along the coastline for 20 kilometres to De Panne near the French border. Heading inland the race takes on a different complexion after the town of Poperinge as riders tackle the 23% cobbled climbs of the Kemmelberg and the Monteberg, difficult enough in the dry but utterly treacherous in the cold wet conditions that often accompany this early season classic. If this were not enough the course then doubles back towards Poperinge forcing the riders to complete this pair of climbs twice. Not surprisingly these "bergs" are often the scene of a defining race winning move. The race then heads east to Menen and then on to finish in the centre of Wevelgem.

Known as a "sprinter's classic" it is not surprising to learn that the most prolific winners of the Gent Wevelgem with three victories apiece are Belgians Robert van Eenaeme, Rick Van Looy and Eddy Merckx and Italian sprinting legend Mario Cipollini.

Paris - Roubaix

Race Facts:
1 Day Race
UCI WorldTour
260km
www.letour.fr

Paris – Roubaix was the brainchild of French businessmen Theodore Vienne and Maurice Perez both of whom had made their fortunes in the textile business. Having financed the new Velodrome in the northern French industrial town of Roubaix the two entrepreneurs set about devising a plan to promote their investment. With the assistance of Victor Breyer, chief editor of the sporting magazine Velo, a plan was hatched to organise a one day race to finish on the track itself under the pretext of it being a training event for the epic 600 kilometre Bordeaux – Paris cycle race held a month later in April.

In the early hours of 19 April 1896, Easter Sunday, 51 riders set off from the Bois-de-Boulogne, Paris. In front of them was 280 kilometres of some of the toughest roads in northern Europe, this inaugural event ultimately being won by Josef Fischer of Germany.

Initially considered a training race, pace-making was allowed until a change in the rules in 1910. These pace-makers were usually fellow cyclists but an unusual precedent was set between 1898 and 1901 when the use of motorcycles and cars for pace-setting was permitted.

Known in its early incarnation as La Pascale, the Easter Race, and then as The Queen of Classics, Paris – Roubaix earned its most famous moniker threading its way through the war ravaged countryside of northern

France in 1919. Surrounded by craters, shattered trees and ruined buildings the term l'enfer du Nord was coined – the Hell of the North.

Paris - Roubaix is synonymous with pave, the cobbles. It was race director Albert Bouvet who originally discovered the 50 kilometres of cobblestones used in the race and persuaded the authorities to leave them in their pre-war condition. Each year the route is slightly modified as race organisers, desperate to retain the character of La Pascale, hunt out remaining stretches of these traditional roads to replace that tarmac-ed over by the highways agencies.

Despite advances in technology and training methods, no cyclist has been capable of beating Dutch cyclist Peter Post who in 1964 set a record average speed of 45.129 km/h. Legendary Belgian Roger de Vlaeminck holds the record for the most Paris – Roubaix victories having taken first place four times between 1972 and 1977. Fabian Cancellara, the brilliant Swiss rider, has lapped up the course in recent years and won his third race in 2013.

Amstel Gold Race

Race Facts:
1 Day Race
UCI WorldTour
250km
www.amstel
goldrace.nl

The Amstel Gold Race was the creation of Herman Krott and Ton Vissers. These two Dutchmen, through their company InterSports were prolific organisers of track and road races within their native Holland. Despite this success they decided to set their sights higher with a grand plan to organise a one-day race to rival the best of the Belgian Classics.

Using his influence with the Amstel Brewery, Krott devised a race to be run from Amsterdam to Maastricht on 30 April 1966 – the birthday of Queen Juliana of the Netherlands. Considering the route too long and complex a revised course was proposed starting in Rotterdam and finishing in the village if Meerssen. Krott's plan to draw the crowds by holding the race on a national holiday almost backfired. With the event already in progress the route had to be changed several times as festivities blocked the roads resulting in a race distance in excess of 300 kilometres.

In its current incarnation the Amstel Gold Race takes the form of three differing circuits based around the city of Maastricht in the province of Limburg. For those who might think the Netherlands a flat country, the race manages to incorporate 31 graded climbs over its 250 kilometres finishing at the summit at Berg en Terblijt.

The Dutch classics specialist Jan Raas holds the record for the most wins having won four times between 1977 and 1980 and then again in 1982.

Flèche Wallonne

The first edition of La Flèche Wallonne, The Walloon Arrow, took place on the roads between Tournai and Liège in 1936 to help promote sales of the Belgian newspaper Les Sports. Over the years the race route and the distance covered has changed considerably but, with the exception of 1940, it has been run every year since its introduction. The race has stayed within the Ardennes region to the east of the country, for a time acting as one half of the classic Weekend Ardennes with Liège Bastogne – Liège.

In its current incarnation the race covers approximately 200 kilometres starting in the Charleroi and then heading east to the infamous 15% climb of the 204 metre Mur de Huy, the Wall of Huy. Riders then embark on a 30km circuit featuring the Côte de Amay followed by a 95 kilometre circuit incorporating a further four tough climbs before heading back to finish at the summit of the Mur.

Belgians Marcel Kint and Eddy Merckx and Italian pair Moreno Argentin and Davide Rebellin are the only four riders to have won the Flèche Wallonne on three occasions. Kints victories are all the more astonishing as they were achieved between 1943 and 1945 in the heart of occupied Europe.

Race Facts:
1 Day Race
UCI WorldTour
200km
www.letour.com

Liège – Bastogne – Liège

Race Facts:

1 Day Race

UCI WorldTour

260km

www.letour.fr

Opposite: The pack rides during the 92th Liege-Bastogne-Liege cycling race between Liege and Ans, April 2006

The oldest race in the professional calendar, Liège – Bastogne – Liège is known to many cycling aficionados as La Doyenne or the old woman. Considered one of the five monuments of cycling, the race was once, alongside Flèche Wallonne, part of Le Weekend Ardennais – a fierce double-header consisting of two of the hardest one day events. The first ever Liège – Bastogne – Liège, won by Belgian amateur Léon Houla, took place in the spring of 1892. Houla remained victorious for the following two years with the race attaining professional status in 1894.

The route south from Liège follows a hilly profile of approximately 95 kilometres to the town of Bastogne, scene of fierce fighting in the closing months of the Second World War. Some riders might be forgiven for thinking that upon reaching this most southerly point of the course half of the racing was done. This is far from the case! The return route of almost 165 kilometres follows an even tougher profile taking in the 11% climbs of the Côte de Saint-Roch, Côte de Stockeu and the Côte de Saint Nicolas with a fair share of cobbles thrown in for good measure.

Whilst the route may be predictable the weather accompanying this Spring Classic is anything but with races having been fought out in everything from blistering 25°C heat to driving sleet and snow. Famously the weather played a major part in the 1957 edition of the race. Contested the previous day, Flèche Wallonne had taken place in the warm air under a clear, blue, sunshine filled May sky. However, overnight a weather front moved in and temperatures dropped dramatically. As the race started in Liège so did the rain, soon turning first to sleet and then to driving snow. As the conditions deteriorated further the retirements came in thick and fast.

A decimated field struggled over the harsh roads north from Bastogne towards Liège. Germain Derycke of Belgium was first to finish but he soon found himself the focus of an enquiry having climbed over the railway crossing gates at Cierreux rather than waiting. Officials declared second placed Frans Schoubben victorious but he was unwilling to take the accolade considering that he had been fairly beaten by his countryman. At the suggestion of Derycke, officials eventually declared both riders to be equal winners.

The most prolific winner of this great race is Eddy Merckx who first took victory in 1969 then consecutively between 1971 and 1973 and again in

1975. Italian Moreno Argentin holds the record for the greatest number of wins by a non-Belgian having won on three occasions between 1985 and 1987 and once more in 1991. Ireland's Dan Martin triumphed brilliantly in 2013.

Tour de Romandie

Race Facts:
Stage Race
UCI WorldTour
630 to 820km
www.tourde
romandie.ch

Right: Winner of the 2006 edition of the Tour de Romandie, Cadel Evans of Australia raises the trophy

The Tour de Romandie, contested in the eastern, French speaking, region of Switzerland, was first run in the summer of 1947 to celebrate the fiftieth anniversary of the Union Cycliste Suisse. Unusually, this stage race, contested in the spring of each year, has never been dominated by a single nation. Swiss riders have only been victorious on twelve occasions in its sixty year history.

The race route changes year to year but invariably starts with a prologue time-trial of approximately 4 kilometres in the city of Geneva and concludes with an individual mountain time-trial starting and finishing at the Stade Olympique in Lausanne. Winding its way across the Jura Mountains and the Alps there can be few races set amongst such a dramatic landscape making the Tour de Romandie a favourite for riders and spectators alike.

With three wins to his name, Irishman Stephen Roche remains the most prolific winner. In 2012 Bradley Wiggins became the first Briton to win the race in the build-up to his Tour de France triumph, before team-mate Chris Froome emulated him en route to winning the centennial Tour in July.

Volta Ciclista a Catalunya

The first edition of the Volta Ciclista a Catalunya, or Tour of Catalonia, took place in the September of 1911. Its undisputed king was Spaniard Mariano Cañardo who won the event three times between 1928 and 1930 and again in 1932, 1935, 1936 and 1939. His seven victories may well have been nine had the event not stopped in 1937 and 1938 due to the Spanish Civil War.

The Tour remained in this autumnal position until 1995 when it was moved to late spring to increase its appeal to riders preparing for the Tour de France. In its current form the first stage takes the unusual shape of a team-time-trial of approximately 20 kilometres, immediately heading for the mountains of the Pyrenees on stage two.

It is truly a race for the mountain goats as every stage without exception includes at least one categorised climb.

The English speaking nations saw good fortune in the mid 1980s with two victories for Ireland's Sean Kelly and one for Scotsman Robert Millar. The great Spaniard Miguel Indurain won three times, while 2013 saw Irish cycling back on the map with success by Dan Martin.

Race Facts:
Stage Race
UCI WorldTour
1000km
www.voltacatalunya.cat

Below: *The pack rides past Bara's arch*

Critérium du Dauphiné Libéré

Race Facts:
Stage Race
UCI WorldTour
1100km
www.criterium.
ledauphine.com

Organised by a regional newspaper of the same name, the Dauphiné Libéré was first run during the summer of 1947 in the Dauphiné region of southeast France. Characterised by its mountainous terrain and featuring numerous major ascents of the Tour de France including the Haute Categorie climbs of Mont Ventoux, Col d'Izoard and Col du Galibier the race is seen, alongside the Tour of Switzerland, as essential preparation for the Tour de France.

All five quintuple winners of the Tour de France have claimed victory in the Dauphiné Libéré on at least one occasion. Jacques Anqutil won the Dauphiné in 1963 and 1965, dominating his eternal rival Raymond Poulidor on both occasions. Eddy Merckx claimed on win from three attempts. His first, in 1971, saw him do battle on the slopes of the Col du Granier with his Spanish adversary Luis Ocaña, winner in 1970, 1972 and 1973. The Belgian returned in 1975 wearing the World Champion's rainbow jersey and again in 1977 but could not repeat his first success.

Bernard Hinault scored his first Dauphiné victory in 1977, defeating previous winner Bernard Thévenet and the great climber Lucien Van Impe. Hinault won again in 1979 and 1980 taking a total of ten stages. Having already won four editions of the Tour de France, Miguel Indurain's winning introduction

to the Dauphiné Libéré came late in his career during the summer of 1995.

Lance Armstrong found himself relegated to the role of lieutenant in 2000 as Tyler Hamilton won for the US Postal team.

Victory would at last come to Armstrong in 2002. Despite finishing fifth in the prologue and second to Columbian Santiago Botero Echeverry during the individual time-trial he took the lead on by crushing the field climbing the Col de Joux Plane on the stage to Morzine. The 2003 Dauphiné would again see Armstrong victorious, despite a heavy fall on stage five. His two wins, though, would a decade later be wiped out.

After four Spanish victories in seven years, 2011 saw the emergence of Bradley Wiggins as a future Tour de France winner. He clinched the biggest win of his career, the first of two consecutive victories, by superbly quelling the threat of Cadel Evans. He became the third Briton to win the traditional Tour warm-up race after Brian Robinson in 1961 and Robert Millar in 1990.

Chris Froome then made it three in a row for Britain before emulating Wiggins by winning his first Tour. Just as Wiggins did in 2012 with teammate Michael Rogers, Australian Richie Porte, Froome's pal and lieutenant, finished overall runner-up, 58 seconds behind.

Tour de Suisse

Race Facts:
Stage Race
UCI WorldTour
1400km
www.
tourdesuisse.
ch

In its contemporary form the Tour of Switzerland is seen by many as the most important stage race on the professional calendar outside of the three Grand Tours. Its combination of fast, flat sprinters stages and high mountains passes is seen, alongside the Critérium du Dauphiné Libéré and Tour of Catalonia, as excellent preparation for the Tour de France. It is fortunate that the professional calendar features three stage races of such high calibre in the weeks prior to the Tour de France allowing the "big guns" of the tour to make their final preparations in relative isolation.

The inaugural five-stage race was won by Swiss rider Max Bulla in the summer of 1933. There followed a period of Italian-Swiss domination, including victories by Ferdi Kubler, Gino Bartali and Hugo Koblet that would last until the 1970s. Only German national champion Hennes Jünkermann was able to break the pattern, taking victory in 1959 and 1962. With four wins to his name Pasquale Fornara of Italy holds the record as the most successful rider in Tour de Suisse history.

Tragedy hit the race on 15 June 1948 during the fourth stage of the Tour from Thun to Altdorf. On the lower slopes of the Süsten Pass Belgians Stan Ockers and Richard Depoorter, in second place on general classification, set off from the peleton in pursuit of escapees Jean Robic of France and race leader Ferdi Kubler of

Switzerland. Cresting the summit the two Belgians were three minutes in deficit of the leading pair. Determined to stay in contention, Depoorter started his descent through the fog towards the valley floor. Traveling at speeds in excess of 90 km/h, he entered one of the many long, unlit tunnels that punctuated the mountain pass. Speeding into the darkness and unable to see his way the Belgian struck the wall and ricocheted into the middle of the road where he then run over and killed by a following car.

American rider Andy Hampsten became the first and only rider to win the Tour of Switzerland in successive years, first in 1986 and then again in 1987 when he took victory by a single second from Dutch mountain specialist Peter Winnen. In more recent years the profile of the race as Tour de France preparation has been all the more evident with Lance Armstrong (the 2001 race now void), Alex Zülle, Alexandre Vinokourov and Jan Ullrich all having taken victory.

ABOVE: Yellow jersey Spain's Koldo Gil Perez rides uphill in front of Germany's Jan Ullrich during the eighth stage of the 70th "Tour de Suisse", June 2006

Deutschland Tour

Race Facts:

Stage Race
1400km
Discontinued
www.
deutschland-
tour.de

The concept of a national cycling tour had existed in Germany from as early as 1911. The race, starting in Breslau (now part of Poland) and finishing in Aachen on the Dutch border was won by Hans Ludwig. Although not in the same league as the Tour de France this inaugural tour was still a considerable challenge taking in Dresden, Erfurt, Nurnberg, Mannheim, Frankfurt and Köln within its six stages and 1500 kilometres. At this time though, the German nation was still split into regional kingdoms and duchies, the resultant organisational difficulties combined with the devestation endured during the First World War prevented the event from achieving any level of consistency from year to year.

Further attempts at a national race were run in 1922, 1927 and 1930 but it was not until the spring of 1931 that the first true Deutschland Tour came into being. Sponsored by the car manufacturer Opel, the 4,046 kilometres race, which was won by German Erich Metze, started and finished in the city of Rüsselsheim. Thirty-six riders from one mixed and five national teams contested the 16 stages, the longest of which was 337 kilometres in length taking almost twelve hours to complete.

Three more Deutschland Tour were organised before the start of the Second World War as the race steadily gained popularity and international standing. The 5,049 kilometres 1939 edition, won

by Georg Umbenhauer, was contested by 68 riders over 20 stages. Starting and finishing in Berlin, its course took the riders first to Breslau in the east then south, through Passau and into the annexed state of Austria and the Alps. It then headed north to Stuttgart, Frankfurt and Köln before heading east to Hannover, Leipzig and Berlin.

Following the war the Tour was reintroduced in the summer of 1947 albeit in a reduced format of just six stages held entirely in the British zone of occupation. Year on year the tour once again grew in stature with the return of the international riders to German soil. In 1950 Roger

Gyselinck of Belgium, with an advantage of nearly eight minutes, became the first non-German to win the Deutschland Tour followed by Italian Guido de Santi the following year.

Sponsorship difficulties meant that the race would be held only sporadically over the next few years, disappearing completely from the calendar in 1962 until its resurrection in the summer of 1979 with funding from Vitamalz, an alcohol free brewery. At last the Deutschland Tour seemed to be living up to expectations with an assembled field of 91 riders including Francesco Moser, Roger de Vlaeminck, Patrick Sercu, Jan Raas and Sean Kelly. The re-born race was won by German Dietrich Thurau of the Ijsboerke-Warncke Eis Team. Further editions were run until the race once again disappeared from view in 1982.

Resurrected, once again, in the summer of 1999 on a wave of German cycling euphoria following the successes of Jan Ullrich, Erik Zabel and the Deutsche Telekom team in the Tour de France, the race found a new August calendar slot avoiding previous clashes with the Giro d'Italia and the pre-Tour de France warm up races.

Despite the rise of German cycling, the sport's links with doping soon put paid to the race. It was disbanded in 2009 as organisers admitted that the doping affairs had hindered finding financial backers.

Clásica Ciclista San Sebastián

In cycling terms the Clásica Ciclista San Sebastian, or San Sebastian Classic, is a relative newcomer to the professional calendar. Held in the undulating countryside of the Basque region of Spain, this 227 kilometre circuit is a climber's heaven featuring a succession of major climbs.

After just 19 kilometres the riders tackle the third category Alto de Orio followed 10 kilometres later by the second category Alto de Garate and then, within another 20 kilometres, the Alto de Azkarate. After another 40 kilometres the summit of the Alto de Udana signals a period of respite for the peleton as there follows the relative ease of 100 kilometres of rolling countryside and coastal roads. The deciding factor of the race arrives after 196 kilometres of racing with the first category climb of the Alto de Jaizkibel just 31 kilometres from the finish.

Since the first edition was won in the autumn of 1981 by Mariano Lejarreta the race has gained in profile becoming a post-Tour de France favourite for many riders. The winner's roster reads like a who's-who of contemporary cycling. Miguel Indurain, Gianni Bugno, Claudio Chiappucci and Lance Armstrong, have all graced the top step of the podium in the short life of this modern classic. There have been seven Spanish winners over the last decade.

Race Facts:
1 Day Race
UCI WorldTour
227km
www.clasica-
san-sebastian.
diariovasco.
com

Eneco Tour

Race Facts:

Stage Race

UCI WorldTour

1230km

www.enecotour.
com

Right: *Australian
Allan Davis cheers
as he finishes
first in Landgraaf
during the Eneco
Tour, August 2005*

The Eneco Tour arrived on the professional cycling calendar comprising of a prologue time-trial and seven road stages across the Netherlands, Belgium and Germany. Sponsored by the Dutch energy company Eneco, the tour made its first appearance in August 2005 having risen from the ashes of the failing Tour of the Netherlands.

The organisers of the Tour of the Netherlands had anticipated inclusion in the inaugural UCI ProTour only to be denied entry with their race being deemed too easy. Undaunted, cooperation was sought from the organisers of the Tour of Belgium and the Tour of Luxembourg with a view of creating an all encompassing Tour.

The 2005 Eneco Tour almost fell into chaos on the fourth stage. Approaching the abbey town of Stavelot the peleton was misdirected by officials whilst a small breakaway group was already ahead on the correct route. Only the intervention police officers forcing the leading riders to stop allowed the race to continue. The excitement continued to the final day as American Bobby Julich of the CSC Team was catapulted from twelfth place on general classification to first with a final stage 26.3 kilometre time-trial of 31'14 to become the winner of the inaugural race.

In recent years, Norway's Edvald Boasson Hagen has twice taken line honours, while Mark Cavendish underlined his potential when he took the points classification in 2007.

Vuelta Ciclista al Pais Vasco

Also known as the Tour of the Basque Country, the first edition of the Vuelta Ciclista al Pais Vasco was won by French cycling legend Henri Pélissier in the summer of 1924. With great international success the Tour continued to feature until 1930 when, with the exception of a single edition in 1935 won by Italian Gino Bartali, it disappeared from the cycling calendar.

Resurrected in the summer of 1969 the first modern Vuelta was won by Tour de France hero Jacques Anqutil. In the 1970s the race was dominated by Spaniard José Antonio Gonzalez Linares who achieved four victories between 1972 and 1979, a record as yet unequalled. Irish King of the Classics Sean Kelly stamped his mark in the mid 1980s by winning three editions between 1984 and 1987 with compatriot Stephen Roche triumphant in 1989.

The Basque Country, entirely mountainous in nature, provides a tough battleground for the professional peleton. Featuring at least one first category climb on each stage, only the very best climbers are able to succeed. In its current format the climax to the race is an individual time trial of approximately 24 kilometres.

Race Facts:

Stage Race

UCI WorldTour

830km

www.
vueltapaisvasco.
diariovasco.com

Left: Riders in the pack climb La Barrerilla hill

Züri - Metzgete

Race Facts:
1 Day Race
241km
Discontinued
www.zueri-
metzgete.ch

The Züri-Metzgete, known also as the Championship of Zurich, had the honor of being the longest contiguously running cycling event in the professional calendar. First held in 1914, when it was won by Henri Rheinwald of Switzerland, the event had been organised annually since 1917 without interruption. That is until the 2007 edition when organisers were forced to cancel the event through lack of sponsorship. Since 2008, the format has seen the name carry on, but as an amateur event.

For many years the Züri-Metzgete was dominated by Swiss riders with foreign nationals only claiming seven victories in the first 41 years of competition. The most famous of these took place in 1946.

Italians Gino Bartali and Fausto Coppi, at the height of their prowess, jointly destroyed the field riding at a blistering pace. It was Bartali who triumphed but in controversial circumstances, attacking whilst Coppi tightened his toe-straps. Their average speed for the race was an astonishing 42.228 km/h, a record that remained unbeaten until 2004.

For much of its existence the Championship of Zurich was held early in the month of May. This was, for many years, a problem for those riders who had contested the Spring Classics of Northern Europe. In 1988 the race was moved to a more rider-friendly August date, encouraging many stars of the Tour de France to participate.

Tour de Pologne

The Tour de Pologne was first organised by the Warsaw Cyclist Association (Towarzystwo Cyklistów w Warszawie) and the Przegl d Sportowy Newspaper in September of 1928. The eight stage race for amateurs, contested by 71 riders over a distance of 1491 kilometres, was won by Feliks Wi cek. Resurrected post war by the Czytelnik publishing house and the Polish Cycling Association, the event was run intermittently until 1952 before taking up a permanent fixture in the cycling calendar although it struggled to gain the international recognition it deserved due to the ruling communist authorities concentrating on the promotion of the Peace Race.

In 1993 the organisation of the Tour de Pologne was passed to Czeslaw Lang, winner of the silver medal at the 1980 Moscow Olympic road race. Under his guidance the race was given professional status by the UCI in 1997.

In its current form, the route of the race covers approximately 1250 kilometres from the Baltic coast in the north to the mountains in the south. From 2006 the traditional final day individual time-trial has been dropped in favour of a road stage in which the riders tackle the 830 metres ascent to the Karpacz summit five times. However the time-trial returned in 2013 when Bradley Wiggins won the 37km final stage.

Race Facts:
Stage Race
UCI ProWorld
1250km
www.
tourdepologne
pl/en

Paris – Tours

Race Facts:
1 Day Race
UCI WorldTour
253km
www.letour.fr

Originally an amateur event, the Paris Tours was first organised in 1896 by the sporting magazine Paris-Vélo. Such was the thirst for cycle sport in France at this time, a crowd of 12,000 anxious spectators packed the Avenue de Grammont in the city of Tours to watch the 42 competitors finish. Unfortunately the sheer numbers of people meant that the road became blocked forcing officials to decide upon the winner on the outskirts of the city. Won by Eugène Prévost the press described this inaugural event as "A crazy, unheard of, unhoped for success." It was though, five years before the event was run for a second time, once again as an amateur event.

The race then suffered another five year absence before being reintroduced in 1906 by a new sponsor, l'Auto, who also organised the Tour de France. With this came a new found status as a professional event, the victory being taken by none other than the great Lucien Petit-Breton.

Through its history the route of the Paris Tours has suffered many changes although the race distance of approximately 250 kilometres has remained fairly constant. The start of the race was soon moved from the centre of Paris to the town of Versailles then following the First World War the route itself was lengthened to include the town of Chinon and the Vallée de

Above:
Germany's Erik Zabel outsprints Italian Daniele Benati in the 2005 Paris-Tours

la Vienne taking the race distance to a massive 342 kilometres. Unpopular with the riders the course reverted to its original route in 1926.

The conditions of the 1921 edition were particularly hard for the riders. Freezing temperatures and fierce blizzards swept across the country forcing half of the field to abandon in the town of Chartres. Late in the race a battle developed between Eugène Christophe and Francis Pélissier. Eventually Pélissier broke clear, taking a lead of several minutes in the atrocious conditions until disaster struck in the form of a puncture. Stranded by the roadside, his hand frozen and unable to repair the tyre, he could but watch as Christophe rode past. Undaunted he proceeded to tear of the damaged tyre using his teeth. Pélissier set off in pursuit. Riding on rim of his wheel he caught his stunned adversary before attacking on the climb of the Azay-le-Rideau to take a stunning solo victory.

Now starting in the little town of Saint Arnould en Yveline, the race has over the years become known as the "Sprinters Classic". Despite many attempts over the years by the organisers to break up the field en-route, the race inevitably results in a mass cavalry charge down the three kilometre arrow straight Avenue de Grammont, though the finish there was disbanded in 2010.

Vattenfall Cyclassics

Race Facts:
1 Day Race
UCI WorldTour
250km
www.vattenfall-cyclassics.de

Originally known as the Hew Cyclassic, the Vattenfall Cyclassic was introduced to the Cycling World Cup in the summer of 1996 as a direct replacement for the failing British organised Leeds Classic and its successor the Rochester Classic, neither of which were considered to measure up to the demands and rigors of world class racing.

Since its introduction the race has gradually gained favour with the riders and public. A relatively low key introduction in 1996 gave way to an impressive event in 1997 with German riders and public alike inspired by the success of Jan Ulrich, Erik Zabel and the Deutsche Telekom team. Ulrich did not disappoint his fans. Fresh from his remarkable victory in the Tour de France he dominated a hard fought race to take victory by seven seconds from a chasing Wilfried Peeters and Jens Hepner. Four years later, six times Tour de France Green Jersey winner Zabel claimed a Hew Cyclassic victory for himself out-sprinting Tour rivals Romans Vansteins and Erik Dekker.

Included as part of the UCI ProTour in 2005, now World Tour, the race underwent a name change in 2006 following the acquisition of HEW (Hamburgische Electricitäts-Werke AG) by European power giant Vattenfall. Prior to the professional race, 20,000 members of the public participate in a fun-ride of 55, 100 or 155 kilometres over the same course.

Eindhoven
Team Time Trial

Conceived as part of the then UCI ProTour, the Eindhoven Team Time Trial is a surprisingly spectacular race from Eindhoven to Helmond and back contested by the 20 ProTour teams and an additional two wild-card entries. Each team of eight riders is set off at intervals of four minutes racing against the clock. The competitors in each team take turns in riding on the front and then "resting" in the slipstream of the others until they fins themselves back on the front of the train once more.

The inaugural event in 2005 was won by the German Gerolsteiner team who averaged 54.414 km/h to cover the course in 53'35", a margin of just three seconds over the second placed Phonak squad.

In its second edition the eight-man Danish based CSC squad including Bobby Julich, Stuart O'Grady, Jens Voigt and David Zabriskie dominated the race from the outset. Passing through each of the intermediate checkpoint in first place they stormed round the 48.6 kilometre course in just 52'28" at an average speed of 55.58 km/h beating the Discovery Channel team into second place by 52 seconds.

Raoc Faotsɪ
1 Day Race
UCI WorldTour
48.6km
www.protour-
eindhoven.nl

Left: *CSC power their way to victory at the 2006 Eindhoven Team Time Trial*

Giro di Lombardia

Race Facts:
1 Day Race
UCI WorldTour
246km
www.gazzetta.
it/Speciali/
GiroLombardia/
en

Known as the "Race of the Falling Leaves", the Giro di Lombardia is the traditional closing event of the professional road cycling calendar. Whilst not Italy's oldest cycling race, predated some twenty-nine years by the Milan-Torino, the Tour of Lombardy was the nation's first international race of note. Since its introduction in 1905 the race has been run every year with the exception of 1943 and 1944.

The inaugural edition was won by Giovanni Gerbi, a resident of Asti who used his local knowledge and some inventive gamesmanship to out-fox his opponents. Appropriately nicknamed the Diavolo Rosso, the Red Devil, Gerbi feigned a minor crash on the approach to a particularly rough and narrow stretch of mountain road. His competitors, seeking to take advantage, immediately attacked totally unaware of the treacherous route ahead. Once his opponents had passed Gerbi climbed back aboard his bike and proceeded to pick his way through the carnage of his crashed adversaries before attacking to take an impressive victory by over 40 minutes.

Early international wins were soon eclipsed by the Italian domination of the race. Following the success of Frenchman Henri Pélissier in 1920 it would not be until compatriot Louison Bobet 's 1950 triumph that a non-Italian rider reign with half of those intervening victories being shard by four riders –

Costante Girardengo, Alfredo Binda, Gino Baratli and the great Fausto Coppi.

In the 1964 edition Briton Tom Simpson attacked early to be countered by Gianni Motta. The two attacked each other mercilessly until Simpson could fight no more allowing the Italian to pedal away to a solo win. The following year, resplendent in the rainbow jersey as world champion, Simpson attacked on the slopes of the Ghisallo but again it was Motta who would track him like a bloodhound. This time though it was the Englishman who would triumph as Motta faded allowing a super-strong Simpson to ride clear.

One of cycle racing's endearing landmarks features on the slopes of the Madonna del Ghisallo, a wooded hillside above Lake Como. At a crossroads near the summit is a small chapel dedicated the Madonna del Ghisallo, patroness of cyclists since 1949 at the behest of Pope Pius XII. The chapel itself is as much a museum as a place of worship containing cycles belonging to Magni, Coppi, Moser, Bartali and Motta, and the jerseys, yellow, pink and rainbow of many a champion past. Italy has not had a winner since 2008.

Above: *Italy's Damiano Cunego (right) grimaces as he crosses the finish line of the "Giro di Lombardia" ahead of Dutch Michael Boogerd, in Como, October 2004*

Critérium International

Race Facts:
Stage Race
300km
www.letour.fr

The Critérium National de la Route was created in the spring of 1932 by Gaston Bénac, sports editor of the Paris-Soir newspaper. Within a short time the race took on the mantle of an unofficial National Championship being contested by the crème de la crème of the French professional peleton. Its original route headed out from Paris on to the southern plains of the Ile de France before heading north to the Vallée de Chevreuse and on to finish in the Parc des Princes velodrome.

As the organisation moved first to the sporting newspaper L'Equipe and then to the Société du Tour de France, the immense popularity of the Critérium National with riders and spectators prompted calls to consider holding the event away from the environs of Paris. During the years of the Second World War two races were organised each year – one in Northern occupied France and one in the unoccupied south.

The role-call of winners for the first 46 years of the Critérium National reads as a who's who of French professional cycling. Leducq, Lapebie, Greves, Idee, Bobet, Hassenforder, Thevenet and Hinault all topped the podium in this most unofficial of National Championships. The constant rivalry between Anquetil and Poulidor was best illustrated by their efforts in the Critérium. Between 1964 and 1962 the two riders each won the race on alternate years with the other

finishing in second place. For once the eternal second got the better of his adversary beating Anquetil five wins to four, a record only equalled by the great wartime rider Emile Idée.

The success of the race had not gone unnoticed and in 1978 the event was opened to foreign riders for the first time becoming the Critérium International. The race continued to build in popularity, taking on a triptych format of two road stages and a time-trial. A relatively flat first stage is followed by a tough hilly second stage that in its current format incorporates nine categorised climbs. The combination of these two differing stages and the final gently rolling eight kilometre time-trial has meant that this race is unique in that it favours no-one.

As an International race an eclectic list of winners includes Zoetemelk, Hinault, Fignon, Kelly, Roche, Indurain, Boardman, Jalabert, Voigt and Froome, continuing the tradition of acting as a showcase for the very best riders in the world.

Omloop Het Volk

Race Facts:
1 Day Race
200km
www.omloophet
nieuwsblad.be

The traditional opening event of the Belgian professional season, this semi-classic was first run in the spring of 1945 by the newspaper Het Volk. Created in reply to the Tour of Flanders organised by rival publication Het Nieusblad, the race quickly established itself as one of the key events on the professional calendar. Although now universally recognised as the Omloop Het Volk the race was, in its formative years, more generally known as Ghent-Ghent due to competitive newspapers refusing to give Het Volk free publicity.

A favourite of the tough Flandrian riders, the Het Volk has only been won by foreign riders on seven occasions. In 1948 the great Fausto Coppi could

well have been the first non-Belgian winner but for a contravention of the rules. Having punctured he took a wheel from a team-mate before chasing down the peleton and riding through to cross the line in first place. However, the regulations of the day precluded the use of outside assistance and the Italian found himself relegated into second place behind Sylvain Grysolle.

It would be further eleven years before, in 1959, Seamus Elliot of Ireland would become the first foreigner to take victory narrowly beating Belgians Alfred de Bruyne and Theo Dingens. It is possible that Elliot could have taken a second victory a year later but in a dispute over the preferential allocation of

race dates the organisers elected to cancel their race in protest.

The weather has always played a major part in the outcome of the Omloop Het Volk. Held on the last weekend in February the race has often been hit by poor weather and it is not uncommon for the organisers to make last minute changes to the route to protect the safety of the riders on the narrow cobbled Flandrian climbs. In the face of this, the weather has only forced one postponement and one cancellation of the race in its long history despite heavy snowfalls prior to the 1955, 1974 and 1988 events.

The route, starting in the East Flandrian capital Ghent, is regarded as one of the toughest in professional cycle racing incorporating many sections of bone-shaking pave and the cobbled climbs of the Oude Kwaremont, Muur de Geraardsbergen, Kleiberg, Eikenberg and Leberg. The race deciding attack is often instigated on the 10% gradient of the vicious Molenberg, a 300 metre long climb 39 kilometres from the finish in Ghent.

Paris – Brest – Paris

Race Facts:
1 Day Race
1200km
Discontinued
www.audax-club-parisien.com

Having witnessed the inaugural 572 kilometre Bordeaux – Paris Pierre Giffard, Editor in Chief of Le Petit Journal was impressed by the interest of the public and the resulting increase in newspaper sales. He had also noted that that the highest placed French rider had placed only fifth behind winning Briton George Pilkington Mills.

Not to be outdone he set about organising a race of his own of enormous magnitude and so was announced the 1200 kilometre Paris-Brest-Paris Cycle Race. The rules were simple and partisan. Only French cyclists were permitted to enter, each rider being permitted the use of ten paid cyclists to assist with draughting and to provide mechanical assistance in the event of mechanical failure or a puncture. The course from Paris followed the "Great West Road", now the Route National 12, through La Queue-en-Yveline, Mortagne-au-Perche, Pré-en-Pail, Laval, Montauban-de-Bretagne, Saint Brieuc and Morlaix. On entering each of these towns the riders were required to stop for a contrôle and have their route book signed and stamped.

No one had any idea how long the race would take or indeed, if it could be finished at all. Inspired by the unknown some 400 riders entered the inaugural race but, with many seeing sense and reason, only 206 riders took to the start line outside the Parisian offices of

Le Petit Journal just before dawn on 8 September 1891. In that first edition Charles Terront, having taken an early lead, punctured near of the town of Laval. Equipped with early clincher tyres he was forced to walk three kilometres to meet his Michelin technicians who then took three-quarters of an hour to change the tyre. Undaunted he battled on before taking the lead as his rival slept during the second night. After 71 hours and 16 minutes without rest Terront eventually crossed the finish line at Port Maillot in Paris to the delight of 10,000 waiting spectators.

The race settled into a cycle of being run once every ten years. As technology and training methods improved so the duration of the race reduced. In its second edition Tour de France champion Maurice Garin brought the winning time down to 51 hours 11 minutes and in the third Emile Georget went 58 minutes faster still.

By the 1930s cycle racing had taken on a different outlook. With professionals concentrating their efforts on the tours and one-day classics the organisers had difficulty in enlisting riders and only 28 competitors lined up at the start. However, the race turned out to be one of the most exciting ever as Frenchman Marcel Bidot, Belgians Leon Louyet, Italian Giuseppe Pancera and Australian Hubert Opperman rolled into the Veleodrome Buffalo at Port Maillot

Above: *Laval, near where Charles Terront had his puncture*

together. After 49 hours 23 minutes of riding the race was decided in a sprint with Opperman taking the verdict from Louyet.

Following the Second World War only two more editions of the PBP would be held. The first, in 1948, was contested by a field of 52 riders and won by Belgian Albert Hendrickx by just half a wheel from compatriot Francois Neuville. The final edition took place during the summer of 1951. In a sprint finish Maurice Diot took

victory from Edouard Muller in a record time of 38 hours 55 minutes having waited after he suffered puncturing 22 kilometres earlier.

Although the professional Paris-Brest-Paris is now consigned to the history books the event lives on as an amateur randonnée held every four years. Whilst this event is not considered a race it has not prevented several riders setting remarkable times. The current amateur course record is an impressive 42 hours 40 minutes.

Bordeaux – Paris

The Bordeaux Paris was first run in 1891, the same year as the inaugural Paris-Brest-Paris it inspired. At 560 kilometres it rated as the longest single day race in the professional cycling calendar, more than double the distance of the Paris-Roubaix. A bizarre feature of the race was that riders were permitted to be paced – initially by tandem-mounted team-mates working in relay then, following 1931, by motorcycles and pedal assisted motorcycles called Dernys.

Organisers predicted the first event would take riders a few days to complete and were surprised when Englishman George Pilkington Mills arrived at the finish in Paris in a little over a day having pedalled through the night without resting. Five years later Arthur Linton, a Welshman from Aberaman, crossed the finish line in first place but, having taken a wrong road in Paris was in danger of disqualification. After an appeal Linton agreed to share his first prize with Frenchman Gastone Rivière. Sadly, two months after his famous victory Linton contracted typhoid and died.

Unfortunately the requirement for specialist training and a clash of dates with the Vuelta a Espana and Giro d'Italia saw the Bordeax-Paris fall from favour. After the last motor-paced race was contested in 1985 and three subsequent un-paced editions failed to attract interest the event was abandoned.

Race Facts:
Bordeaux –
Paris
1 Day Race
600km
Discontinued
www.
bordeauxparis.
com/en

World Road Championship

Race Facts:
One Day
Championship
260km
www.uci.ch

After the Grand Tours, the World Road Championship is the most coveted of titles in the professional cycling calendar. For many years the Worlds were held in the month of August, encouraging riders fresh with form from the Tour de France to compete but, in 1995, the governing UCI made a decision to move the Championship to a later date in October. Many feared that this change would result in depleted fields of lower quality riders but, with the Vuelta a España having similarly moved from its traditional April slot to September, the race remains as hard fought as ever.

With the World Track Championships having enjoyed five years success, it was in 1898 that the concept of an equivalent road championship was mooted. It would though take another twenty-three years and the lobbying of the Italian Federation before the race would come into fruition. The first World Road Championship, won by Swede Gunnar Skold, was an amateur event that took place in 1921 as a 190 kilometre time-trial based around the city of Copenhagen before moving to a conventional road race format two years later.

In 1927, influenced once more by the Italians, a professional championship was introduced alongside the amateur event. The inaugural edition, held at the Nurburgring in the north of Germany, was appropriately won by the 25 year old Italian Alfredo Binda who would take further victories at Liege in 1930 and then on home turf two years later in Rome.

When the Belgian selectors realised that the 1934 Championship in Leipzig has to be held on a completely flat course they despatched track endurance specialist Karel Kaers. Their unconventional planning proved a success as Kaers dominated the race, maintaining such a high speed that any chance of an escape became impossible.

The only annual event that sees competitors replace their professional jerseys with that of their nation, one of the issues of the World Road Championship is always the conflict of loyalty between team and country. This first became apparent as the race moved to Valkenberg in 1938. Having won the Tour de France, Italy's Gino Bartali was considered the outstanding favourite to become World Champion but his hopes were dashed as his countrymen Mario Vicini and Aldo Bini failed to wok for him allowing their professional team leader, Belgian Marcel Kint, to take victory.

Following seven years of absence due to the Second World War, the Championship returned to the professional calendar in 1946 to yet more controversy. Held in Zürich, victory went to home-

Above: Spain's Team with Oscar Freire (left) rides during the elite road race of the 2004 UCI road world championships in Verona.

nation rider Hans Knecht who escaped on the final climb to the finish to win by 10 seconds from 1938 Champion Kint who claimed that a hand had grabbed his saddle in the final sprint denying him the win.

The 1948 edition was expected to host a battle royal between the Italian greats Fausto Coppi and Gino Bartali but, as the eventual winner, Belgian Brik Schotte, slipped away with the Frenchmen Apo Lazarides and Lucien Teisseire, the feuding duo were left watching each other at the back of the peleton. For Coppi and Bartali it was more important that the other loose than they should win. For their trouble the pair were suspended from competition for three months.

Coppi eventually won his World Championship in 1953 in a race torn apart from constant attacks by the Luxembourgian Charly Gaul. Of the seventy starters only twelve remained in contention with 80 kilometres remaining at which point the Italian Campionissimo attacked to take a solo victory 6'22" ahead of second placed Germain Derijcke of Belgium.

The following year found Coppi hunting for a second victory as the race moved to the German city of Solingen. Early in proceedings a break formed, instigated by Frenchman Robert Varnajo and Michele Gismondi of Italy who were soon joined by Louison Bobet, Jacques Anquetil, Fritz Schär, Gaul and Coppi. The tempo was vicious and the group was soon reduced as first Varnajo, Gismondi and Anquetil were unable to maintain the pace and then Coppi spun his wheel on the climb. Gaul was next to fall by the wayside leaving Bobet and Schär to fight for victory. As the pair rode past the pits on the last lap, with the team mechanics already packing away, Bobet punctured. A fast thinking mechanic sprinted down the circuit, wheel in hand, and within moments the Frenchman was away again but the Swiss was already gone.

Bobet pressed on, gradually reeling in the brave, lone Schär before catching passing his adversary on the final climb to take victory by 12 seconds.

Van Steenbergen added to his 1949 victory by taking World Championship honours again in 1956 and 1957 with his countryman and Rival Rik Van Loy winning consecutively in 1960 and 1961. Contested in 1962 at the Italian town of Salo, Frenchman Jean Stablinski took a notable victory from Seamus Elliott of Ireland. Having successfully broken away from the peleton the race looked to be his until, on the last lap and away from the pits, he punctured. Undeterred, Stablinski borrowed a bicycle several sizes too large from a spectator and continued on to finish 1'22" clear.

An exciting sprint between Germany's Rudi Altig and British hero Tom Simpson brought the 1965 Championship to a satisfying conclusion. The two friends, who had worked well together after breaking clear of the lead group, agreed that with one kilometre remaining they would separate and ride their own, unassisted race to the line. With tears in his eyes, Simpson crossed the line in first position to take Britain's first World Championship victory. However, compensation cold be found for Altig the following year when he took the championship from Jacques Anquetil and Raymond Poulidor in front of a home crowd at Germany's Nurburgring.

In 1967 a five up sprint was won by Eddy Merckx in what would be his first of three World Championship titles. His second rainbow jersey came four years later on the road of Mendrisio in Switzerland in a race so dominated by the Belgian that only the Italian Felice Gimondi could match his pace. A third title was gained in 1974 when the Championship left Europe to be contested in Montreal, Canada.

With a palmares that already included victories in the Tour, Giro and Vuelta in addition to the Pernod Super-Prestige title much was expected of Bernard Hinault at the 1980 World Championship. Hinault's performance was far from disappointing. Undeniably the strongest rider in the race, he attacked on the same climb each lap until, one by one, his opposition was demolished leaving him to time-trial solo to the finish line in one of the most decisive Championship victories ever.

American Greg Lemond took a popular victory at the 1983 Championship after destroying Spaniard Faustino Ruperez in the final kilometres to become the first

non-European to win the title. Lemond repeated the achievement in 1989, his first year back in competition after receiving serious shotgun injuries in a hunting accident.

Stephen Roche achieved the seemingly impossible in 1987 when, having already won the Giro d'Italia and the Tour de France earlier in the year, he overcame incessant marking to become only the second rider ever to take cycling's Triple Crown. With less than a lap remaining a small group, including the Irishman, went clear. With sprinter team-mate Sean Kelly closely marked by defending champion Moreno Argentin, Roche attacked and, with 500 metres remaining, rocketed past a surprised bunch to take victory by a single second from the Italian.

The versatile Gianni Bugno then came to the fore for a sublime double success in 1991 and 1992. He first held off Steven Rooks of the Netherlands before beating Laurent Jalabert the following year. Lance Armstrong won the race in 1993.

The Sicilian based 1994 World Championships heralded the introduction of an elite men's time trial to complement the road title. In its first edition, victory was taken by British Olympic pursuit champion Chris Boardman with Italian

Andrea Chiurato in second place and Jan Ulrich In third with the corresponding road title being won by Frenchman Luc Leblanc.

The 1995 Championships were an all Spanish affair dominated by just two riders. Victory in the time-trial went to Tour de France superstar Miguel Indurain with the silver medal being taken by countryman Abraham Olano. The result was reversed in the road race as Olano broke clear on the final lap to finish solo albeit with a flat rear tyre after having punctured on the final descent into Duitama.

Spaniard Oscar Freire took his first world title in 1999 but controversy surrounded the result of his 2001 win in Lisbon, Portugal when Mapei rider Paolo Lanfranchi seemingly chased down his countryman Gilberto Simoni, leader of the rival Saeco team, allowing Freire, his professional team leader, to ride away to victory. Freire claimed his third title three years later when the championship returned to Italian roads in a sprint finish with German Erik Zabel.

By winning the 2005 World Road Championship 24 year old Belgian sprinter Tom Boonen capped a remarkable year that had included two Tour de France stage wins, Paris Roubaix and the Tour of Flanders.

Italian Paolo Bettini just fell short that year, but elation soon followed with a double success in 2006 and 2007. In 2010 came the turn of Mark Cavendish, continuing British cycling's remarkable rise. The Isle of Man rider won in a tight sprint and thus became the first British world champion since Tom Simpson in 1965.

After Tour de France success the past two years, Britain was well set for more world honours in the 2013 Championships in Florence. The day, though, was beset by problems as rain scuppered any hopes of success. It was left to Rui Costa to take gold. However, the race will be remembered for Vincenzo Nibali's efforts. Having already crashed badly, the Italian somehow got back to the leaders but finished in an agonising fourth.

Olympic Road Race

Cycling is one of the few sports that has featured at every Olympic Games since they were established in 1896 although over the years the format has varied.

At the Games of 1896 competitors raced from Athens to Marathon at which point they stopped to sign their name on a check sheet before remounting and returning to Athens, a total of 87 kilometres. The winner on that occasion was Aristidis Konstantinidis of Greece.

Cycling continued to feature on the Olympic programme, but it was not until the Berlin Games of 1936 that the road race returned, won by Frenchman Robert Charpentier. The 1956 Olympics was won by Ercole Baldini after the start was delayed fifteen minutes when it was realised that two impostors were present within the peleton. Butcher Tom Gerard and carpenter Paul Fitzgerald had travelled from their native Ireland to protest in support of the IRA. In 1956 Baldini had already won the 4,000 metres pursuit at the World Championship and set a new Hour Record. Turning professional in 1957, his career continued to go from strength to strength as he took wins in both the World Road Championship and the Giro d'Italia.

Winner of the 1992 Olympic Road Race at the Barcelona Games was twenty-one year old Italian Fabio Casartelli who escaped on the penultimate lap with

Race Facts:
One Day
Championship
240km
www.olympic.
org

Dutch rider Erik Dekker and Latvian Dainis Ozols before sprinting clear in the last 250 metres. Tragically, three years later the popular Italian died of his injuries after crashing on the decent of the Portet-d'Aspet during the Tour de France.

After 100 years of competition, the 1996 Atlanta Games were the first in which professional riders were permitted to compete. Whilst training in the days leading up to race, Briton Max Sciandri and Swiss rider Pascal Richard met with Rolf Sørensen of the Danish team who offered to show them the course. The following week the three riders were together again as the winning break in the Olympic Road Race with Richard taking victory from Sørensen with Sciandri in third place.

The result at the 2000 Games owed as much to professional loyalties as it did to national honour. With 25 kilometres remaining, Jan Ullrich broke clear of the lead group accompanied by compatriot Andreas Klöden and Alexander Vinokourov of Kazakhstan. The three rode well together until, in the final kilometres, Ullrich calmly rode clear to take the gold medal followed moments later by Vinokourov and Klöden – an

Left: *Cyclists
head off at the
start of the men's
cycling road
race during the
Athens 2004
Summer Olympic
GamesIndividual
(100km) event,
1936*

Oppostie: *French
champion Robert
Charpentier poses
after winning tho
gold medal in the
Berlin Olympic
Road Race
Individual (100km)
event, 1936*

unsurprising result for three members
of the German sponsored Deutsche
Telekom team.

A big crash early in proceedings at
the 2004 Games had an impact on the
results, before Italian Paulo Bettini
who took the gold medal from Sergio
Paulinho or Portugal.

At the 2008 Games in Beijing,
Samuel Sánchez edged out a host of
names in a six-man sprint to win gold.

Four years later, Alexandr Vinokurov
outsprinted Rigoberto Uran Uran to
upset the odds on the streets of London.
The Olympics were supposed to be
paved with golden success on the roads,
with Bradley Wiggins, Mark Cavendish
and Chris Froome in the field, but they
finished well down the field. Marianne
Vos, of the Netherlands, then held
off – agonisingly for home fans - Lizzy
Armitstead in a sprint finish.

**The pictures in this book were provided
courtesy of the following:**

GETTY IMAGES
101 BAYHAM STREET, LONDON NW1 0AG

WIKICOMMONS
commons.wikimedia.org

Design and artwork by Scott Giarnese

Published by G2 Entertainment Limited

Publishers Jules Gammond and Edward Adams

Written by Jon Stroud and Rod Gilmour